Elite • 192

# World War II Tactical Camouflage Techniques

279921

**GORDON L. ROTTMAN**

ILLUSTRATED BY PETER DENNIS
*Series editor Martin Windrow*

First published in Great Britain in 2013 by Osprey Publishing,
Midland House, West Way, Botley, Oxford, OX2 0PH, UK
43-01 21st Street, Suite 220B, Long Island City, NY 11101, USA
E-mail: info@ospreypublishing.com

OSPREY PUBLISHING IS PART OF THE OSPREY GROUP

A CIP catalog record for this book is available from the British Library

Print ISBN: 978 1 78096 274 0
PDF ebook ISBN: 978 1 78096 275 7
ePub e-book ISBN: 978 1 78096 276 4

Editor: Martin Windrow
Index by Rob Munro
Typeset in Sabon and Myriad Pro
Originated by PDQ Media, Bungay, UK
Printed in China through Worldprint Ltd

13 14 15 16 17 18 10 9 8 7 6 5 4 3 2 1

Osprey Publishing is supporting the Woodland Trust, the UK's leading
woodland conservation charity, by funding the dedication of trees.

**www.ospreypublishing.com**

## IMPERIAL WAR MUSEUM COLLECTIONS

Many of the photos in this book come from the Imperial War Museum's
huge collections, which cover all aspects of conflict involving Britain and
the Commonwealth since the start of the 20th century. These rich resources
are available online to search, browse and buy at HREF= . In addition to
Collections Online, you can visit the Visitor Rooms where you can explore
over 8 million photographs, thousands of hours of moving images, the
largest sound archive of its kind in the world, thousands of diaries and
letters written by people in wartime, and a huge reference library. To make
an appointment, call (020) 7416 5320, or e-mail mail@iwm.org.uk

## ACKNOWLEDGMENTS

The author wishes to thank Tom Laemlein of Armor Plate Press and Nik
Cornish at STAVKA for their photographic support.

## ARTIST'S NOTE

Readers may care to note that the original paintings from which the color
plates in this book were prepared are available for private sale. All
reproduction copyright whatsoever is retained by the Publishers. All
enquiries should be addressed to:

Peter Dennis, Fieldhead, The Park, Mansfield, Nottinghamshire NG18 2AT,
UK

The Publishers regret that they can enter into no correspondence upon this
matter.

## LINEAR MEASUREMENTS

Distances, ranges, and dimensions are given in the contemporary US
system of feet, yards, and statute miles rather than metric. To convert
these figures to metric the following conversion formulas are
provided:

feet to meters

multiply feet by 0.3058

yards to meters

multiply yards by 0.9144

miles to kilometers

multiply miles by 1.6093

# CONTENTS

# WORLD WAR II TACTICAL CAMOUFLAGE TECHNIQUES

## INTRODUCTION

Use of Camouflage. *Camouflage uses concealment and deception to promote our offensive action, to surprise, to mislead the enemy, and to prevent him from inflicting damage upon us. Concealment includes hiding from view, making hard to see clearly, arranging obstructions to vision, deceiving and disguising, and deception involving sound.* (US Field Manual FM 5-20, 1944)

Camouflage is about breaking up outlines rather than complete concealment, which is seldom possible. In thawing weather or areas of spotty snow, solid over-white suits were "too white." Here a US infantryman has painted irregular whitewash bands on his olive drab uniform and helmet. Note that he has not painted his M1 rifle. (Tom Laemlein/Armor Plate Press)

Through many centuries in the history of warfare, camouflage was of little concern. Armies maneuvered in precise linear formations and faced one another in massed blocks, adorned in colorful uniforms. Large bodies of troops were usually impossible to conceal; on the march they left broad trails of trampled mud or kicked up clouds of summer dust, and when they bivouacked they lit countless smoky fires. The threat of aerial observation did not exist, and the only means of detecting the enemy was line-of-sight observation. Foot patrols were short-ranged, with no means of reporting information until they returned to their lines. Cavalry were the true "commander's eyes," since they had the capability to reconnoiter deeply and could report more timely information owing to their speed – but they too had to dispatch couriers to carry their reports physically.

After a brief transitional period at the turn of the 19th to 20th centuries, when longer-ranged rifles forced some armies to issue drab-colored clothing, it was World War I that changed warfare and the nature of the battlefield forever. The means of detecting the enemy multiplied. Weapons were no longer limited by comparatively short range and direct fire, and longer-ranged, more lethal, rapid-fire weapons ruled the battlefield. Units had to maneuver dispersed, burrow into the ground, and camouflage themselves from observers both on the ground and in airplanes and tethered balloons. When detected, the enemy's location and other information could be relayed to artillery and machine guns by telephone and even radio, and the fire could be adjusted by the same means. Camouflage became essential to hide from and mislead the enemy,

and to disguise activities and installations. This book focuses on tactical camouflage – those techniques used by frontline units – as practiced in World War II by the US, British Commonwealth, Soviet and German forces. It does not detail the specifics and changes over time of armored fighting vehicle (AFV) and aircraft camouflage schemes, which are studies in their own right (see Osprey's New Vanguard series and our various aviation series). Nor does it address major higher-echelon camouflage projects, such as concealing entire airfields, making aircraft factories look like suburban neighborhoods, or creating decoy harbors complete with dummy ships.

# PRINCIPLES OF CAMOUFLAGE

Battlefield camouflage was one of many tactical techniques and skills essential for survival and for the conduct of successful combat operations, both offensive and defensive. Camouflage at the tactical level (division and below) was a standard procedure for all armies – but it was one that was often poorly taught, with little training time allocated. It was generally expected that minimal skills would be taught and that units would integrate camouflage practices into tactical training. With so many simultaneous tasks to be undertaken by field units, camouflage practices were often neglected. It was soon learned in combat that camouflage was absolutely essential, owing to the range and lethality of modern weapons, aerial reconnaissance, and increased ground reconnaissance capabilities all found in modern mobile warfare.

The individual camouflage that can be adopted by line infantry, who have to be capable of movement across country, is quite different from the more elaborate "ghillie suits" and other measures devised by snipers, who have to remain static for many hours in concealment sophisticated enough to frustrate ground observers who are actively searching for them with binoculars at short to medium range. Some wartime photos were released to the press showing rather over-theatrical techniques; this one shows two British riflemen in the UK during the 1940 invasion scare, draped in "wire wool." Apart from its impracticality for men who have to move around, and its cost, as made from a strategic material, it has the drawback that Spanish moss is not found in English autumn woodlands. (Imperial War Museum H5464)

These US tents and a workshop truck have been well concealed by drape nets to blend into the edge of a Normandy wood. This may be a maintenance unit, but headquarters, supply, and other support units appeared similar. (Tom Laemlein/Armor Plate Press)

Regardless of which army, basic camouflage principles, techniques, and materials were similar. Despite what the manuals and directives specified, however, soldiers used whatever materials were available, fabricated their own means and created their own techniques to suit circumstances, local terrain, and climate conditions. The use of substitute materials and techniques was common.

US Field Manual FM 5-20, *Camouflage, Basic Principles* (1944) described features of camouflage and how they contributed to concealment, or failed to do so:

*a. Form.* Man-made objects or groups of objects tend to have straight or uniformly curved lines and are laid out in regular patterns, while nature tends to form irregular patterns. In an area of irregularity, a regular object attracts attention. If the object is of a military nature, it will be conspicuous to the enemy. Its shape and its relative size are clues to its identity.

*b. Shadow.* From the air, shadows are very noticeable, particularly on aerial photographs. Often a shadow reveals the form of an object better than its top outline. Objects such as factory chimneys, telegraph poles, vehicles, and tents, for example, have distinctive shadows. Objects in the shadow of another object are more likely to be overlooked.

*c. Texture. (1)* Texture is the degree of roughness of a surface. A rough surface has the ability to cast shadows within itself. Perfectly smooth surfaces cast no shadow, absorb no light, and therefore have smooth texture. From such surfaces a large proportion of the reflected light rays enter the eye or the camera, and the surface appears light. Barren or rocky surfaces having no vegetation reflect most of the light they receive; they have little texture and appear light gray when photographed. *(2)* Surfaces which contain large numbers of shadows, such as grass and brush or heavy woods, absorb light; they have much texture. They reflect very little light and appear dark on photographs. The degree of darkness is largely dependent upon the amount of texture. For instance, a field of tall grass will appear darker in a photograph than a field of short grass, since the former has a greater shadow content than the latter.

*d. Color.* Color differences at close range distinguish one object from another.

*e. Movement.* The area in view below an aerial observer is so large that small objects fade into the landscape and do not attract his eye. If the object moves, however, the eye is immediately attracted, and what was unnoticed is suddenly conspicuous. The aerial camera records the fact that something has moved when two photographs of the same area are taken with a time interval between. If an object has moved, the changed position is apparent when the two photographs are compared. The same principles hold true in ground observation.

## Definitions

The term "camouflage" (German, *Tarn*; Russian, *kamuflyaj*; Italian, *mimetizzazione*) covers a broad area of concealing, disguising, deceiving, altering, and obscuring military activities, facilities, troops, equipment, and matériel. (Incidentally, the abbreviations "camo" or "cammie" were not used during World War II.) Not only does camouflage conceal or hide, but it strives to break up or alter the familiar structural lines and appearance of objects, to mislead as to what the object is or give the impression that it is something else; it prevents the enemy from determining what activity is taking place or its extent, and makes it difficult to estimate range. Camouflage can be a stratagem or scheme to conceal, deceive, or disguise in conjunction with the use of deceptive measures such as dummy and decoy equipment and positions. Camouflage also serves to delay the recognition of a target and impede engagement; it can cause an enemy gunner or pilot to be deceived or confused, thus either preventing an attack or at least causing it to be inaccurate.

The physical aspect of camouflage includes the use of appropriately colored paints applied in disruptive patterns on vehicles, facilities, structures, equipment, and just about anything else. It also includes garnished nets, screens, natural materials, and the use of mottled uniforms and gear. Camouflage is not always intended to completely hide an object, since this is seldom possible, but is constructed to deceive the human eye by altering the perceived shape of regular and familiar forms by obscuring their distinctive features and regular outlines.

## Cover, and concealment – sight, sound and smell

Two terms often seen in military discussions are "cover" and "concealment." They are not one and the same thing.

"Cover" describes something that offers protection from direct observation and fire. This could be as small as a foxhole, ditch, wall, or fallen tree; a building, air raid shelter, or armored fighting vehicle; or a major feature such as the crest of a hill or ridge, covering the reverse slope (the side away from the enemy). Cover may conceal one from direct observation, but does not necessarily deny the enemy knowledge of one's presence. The crew of an AFV may be "under cover" in the sense of being behind steel plate, but their presence is obviously known if the tank is advancing in the open. A foxhole may offer cover from fire, but the enemy may at least assume the position is occupied from the fact that its uncamouflaged parapet is visible. Cover from direct ground fire might not offer cover from the plunging indirect fire of artillery or mortars, let alone from aerial attack. "Cover" might also mean simply "concealment," as in the order to "stay under cover," meaning to remain under trees or other concealment to avoid ground or air detection.

With the wax-pencil marks made by the RAF photo interpreter still visible, this vertical aerial shot was taken at night using a "flash bomb," apparently from no more than 1,000 feet up. It shows German towed artillery on the move on the Dutch-German border in winter 1944/45. Note that while not exactly identifiable, the camouflaged structures at upper left are clearly visible. (IWM CL1855]

"Concealment" means to be hidden from observation by the enemy, but not necessarily protected (covered) from fire. Concealment may be gained by hiding behind foliage, terrain features, buildings, walls, etc. It can also be achieved by the use of camouflage clothing, vehicle pattern-painting, camouflage nets, or the application of natural materials, in order to blend into surroundings or the background. When faced by aerial observation, a man's "background" is not only behind him, but also beneath him; it is critical to blend into the background from every angle, and "all-round concealment" – that is, to be hidden from aerial observation and 360-degree ground observation – is difficult to achieve.

Simple movement by vehicles and troops was what most frequently attracted the enemy's attention, no matter how well concealed; movement, even slight, naturally attracts the eye. The effective selection of movement routes is essential to maintaining concealment; this might involve moving along streambeds, ditches, and gullies, keeping screening vegetation between you and the enemy, staying behind walls and buildings, avoiding open areas, and staying off skylines to prevent oneself being silhouetted. Concealment, at least in the short term, can be achieved by the use of smoke-screens, the darkness of night, and weather conditions: rain, sleet, snow, fog, and dust. These are only temporary conditions, and the tactical situation may not allow soldiers to take advantage of them at the time they occur.

Other factors that have to be considered for effective camouflage include "noise discipline" – voices, weapons firing, equipment sounds, and vehicle noises; in the frontlines vehicle horns are often disconnected. Noise discipline also entails soldiers silencing their equipment and weapons so that they do not knock together, since such sounds carry, particularly on a still night. The firing of weapons reveals positions by sound, but also by muzzle-flash, smoke, raised dust, or the back-blast of a rocket or recoilless weapon. "Light discipline" means avoiding the unnecessary use of lights, and ensuring that necessary lights are concealed. Vehicle lights, flashlights (torches) and lanterns, cooking/warming fires, and cigarettes are the main culprits.

Such signatures as dust raised by vehicles and marching troops, vehicle exhaust smoke, the smoke of cooking/warming fires, even the steam of massed soldiers breathing in extreme cold conditions can give away activity. Undisciplined discarding of ammunition packing cases and materials, cartridge cases, ration containers, and other trash can betray otherwise camouflaged positions; it does little good to expertly camouflage an artillery gun pit while leaving crew equipment, drying laundry, ammunition boxes, and expended shell cases lying exposed. Disturbed soil and vegetation and construction debris also reveal positions. Likewise, disturbed and cut vegetation used elsewhere for camouflage can be revealing, as can vegetation cleared for fields of fire. Vehicle tracks and footpaths made by troops, and mud stirred up in the water after a stream has been crossed, are easily detected from the air and sometimes by distant ground observers. "Shine" – reflected light, from binoculars, optical weapon sights, vehicle windshields, windows and headlight lenses – can attract the enemy's attention from long distances.

At the other end of the scale, the sense of smell is also useful on the battlefield. The characteristic smells of cooking food, warming fires, vehicle fuel and exhaust, burnt artillery propellant, trash fires, and smoking tobacco may all be detected at short distances.

## Natural cover – woodland

Natural cover will often mean woods, but an extract from the British military training pamphlet *Camouflage, Part 1: General Principles: Equipment and Materials (all Arms)* points out some drawbacks to be considered:

1. The best interests of concealment as well as the best tactical interests are by no means always served by the use of the natural cover of woods. These are not only already suspect, but the cover afforded is often less than it appears.
2. It is worth while remembering that the efficiency of cover in woods depends greatly upon the sun. In strong sunlight it is much harder for the observer to pierce the cover of the leaves, and even bare branches are endowed by the sun with shadows that spread a protecting pattern over all who seek concealment. [Another factor is that troops without overhead cover in woods are endangered by artillery and mortar airbursts in the treetops.]
3. Positions sited in woods in summer tend to develop an unnecessary amount of unconcealed works: men's quarters, cookhouse, etc.

The result of this false sense of security may be serious when winter comes. In the case of artillery, guns sited on the edge of a wood are liable to be discovered because the dark background shows up not only the flash but also the smoke, which in the open would disperse more quickly. Better cover, in that it lends itself less readily to identification, can be found in tall hedges, while a broken background of heath or scrub can always be improved so as to afford admirable concealment. For some cases the concealment afforded by a good background is better and also more permanently reliable than that given by overhead cover.

That said, in the vast forested areas of Northwest Europe, Russia, Eastern Europe, and other regions it was of course necessary to operate in woods. Troops learned not to emplace defenses on the outer edge of woods, but deep in the forest. This denied enemy observers direct surveillance, forced attackers to advance slowly, limited the use of armor, and allowed defenders essentially to ambush the attackers from well concealed positions.

## Enemy observation capabilities

Visual observation is by far the most common means of detecting activity, facilities, positions, and whatever else is attempted to be camouflaged.

Ground observation could be maintained for long periods, although its range and effectiveness were greatly decreased at night. Ground observers increased their range of vision with binoculars, telescopes, and optical weapon sights. Hearing-range and direction accuracy could be increased by sound-ranging equipment, but this was limited to artillery target acquisition units. During World War II there was no effective portable ground surveillance radar, and infrared night vision devices were in their infancy.

Aerial observation was either visual or photographic. Reconnaissance aircraft could only loiter over an area of interest for a limited time, and additional flights were intermittent. Aerial observers and aerial photographs provided only a "snapshot" of what was occurring at the time of the flyover, and the information diminished in value, to a greater or lesser extent, during the time it took to reach the relevant ground commander. The recon aircraft had to return to base, reports had to be made and photographs developed; the information took time to analyze, and was then passed down "through channels." It might be days old by the time ground units received it.

Haze, fog, rain, snow, low clouds, dust, smoke, antiaircraft fire, and interference by enemy aircraft all limited the effectiveness of aerial observation – to say nothing of the darkness of night, which was when the enemy was most active. Visual aerial observation might be able to detect activity and positions so that attack aircraft and/or artillery could fire on targets. Photographic aerial observation was usually more revealing, because it permitted longer and more detailed study of the target area and terrain. Panchromatic, infrared, and color film all aided in the detection of camouflage. However, the Axis forces had little or nothing in the way of such capabilities. Through much of the war the Axis achieved only limited air superiority. Although this was notable during the 1940–41 Blitzkrieg campaigns, and still a significant threat in North Africa and Italy, after 1943 their tactical aerial photographic and even visual aerial observation of the battlefield was limited. Conversely, of course, with the Allied achievement of air superiority, camouflage from aerial reconnaissance and attack became ever more major concerns for the Germans.

# CAMOUFLAGE MATERIALS

## Paint

Virtually all metal military equipment – from entrenching tools, to helmets, to radio sets, to AFVs – were painted to protect the surface from the weather, preventing rusting and corrosion, and for camouflage. The paints used were normally matt (flat –"lusterless," in US parlance) for low reflectivity. Each army had a standard paint for their base color, although there were alternative colors, changes in authorized shades, and additional colors available for camouflaging. These basic colors were: US, olive drab (green, with brown predominating); UK, bronze green (dark green); USSR, olive green (varied greatly from brownish to green shades).

Germany used gray (*grau*) for AFVs, but field gray (*feldgrau*, anything from mid gray-green to dark olive green) was also used for other vehicles and equipment. From 18 February 1943, in order to conserve green pigment and provide a light base color on which to paint darker camouflaging color patterns, vehicles, large weapons, and other items of ordnance equipment were factory-painted dark yellow (*dunkelgelb*).

Large ammunition items such as bombs, mines, hand and rifle grenades, artillery projectiles, mortar rounds, rockets, demolition charges, etc, were usually painted with a camouflaging color along with other colored markings and bands for identification of type. This allowed bombs stacked beside airstrips, mortar rounds lying ready on the edge of a pit, hastily laid unburied mines, and ammunition items handled by soldiers at the front to be less conspicuous while still quickly recognizable.

An example of US munitions shows how an identifying color was changed to provide more effective camouflage. Prior to 1943, US high-explosive munitions were painted lusterless yellow, a logical peacetime choice: it served as a cautionary warning, and made it easy to locate duds and lost munitions. The change from yellow to olive drab was directed in late 1942 and fully implemented on new munitions by early 1943. Yellow Mk II hand grenades hanging on a soldier's web gear drew unwanted attention, and Marines on Guadalcanal quickly realized another drawback. The Japanese could easily find a yellow grenade tossed into their position at night, as the color stood out even in minimal illumination, and this sometimes allowed them time to throw the grenade back. Grenades in service were often repainted olive drab by ordnance refurbishment units.

Armies authorized several standard colors to camouflage-paint vehicles, large equipment items, structures, etc. Early in the war two-color patterns were used, generally a lighter base color with a darker disruptive color. Three- and occasionally four-color patterns were later introduced. These included various shades of green and brown including a wide range of drabs, earth-reds and yellows, black, tan, sand, and gray. Gray was often an under-used color; close observation shows that many treetrunks are more gray than brown, and gray also blends into fog, mist, smoke, and shadows deep within foliage. Black was sometimes over-used; it appears little in nature, and shadows are seldom that dark.

## Vehicles

Often, official patterns were specified for particular models or types of vehicles, while the exact shades for the different parts of the pattern were to be selected by the unit, based on local vegetation and soil plus seasonal considerations.

An example from the Eastern Front, 1943–44, of the two main approaches to camouflage-painting of fighting vehicles: a British Churchill tank supplied to the Red Army and painted solid olive green, and an abandoned German Sd Kfz 232 heavy armored car with pattern-painting over factory dark yellow finish. Compare the patterning on the nose shield with Plate G3.

It was not uncommon for standard patterns to be ignored or modified to suit local conditions, or simply because of the painter's artistic flair. Again, units might advance, withdraw or be relocated over great distances; the terrain and vegetation coloration and patterns changed, sometimes drastically, but often units did not have the time or the materials to repaint their vehicles and equipment.

Model-builders often agonize over the exact "official" colors of AFV paints (see also below, chapter "Vehicle Camouflage"). The reality is that few of the colors actually used in the field exactly matched official color swatches. Even factory-applied base paints varied depending on factory and time frame. In the field, paints were often diluted with paint thinner or gasoline to stretch limited supplies, and other colors were mixed in for the same reason, or to achieve shades better matching local coloration.

The Germans issued paint in paste form, and its shade varied depending on what type and how much thinner was used. It also depended on how the paint was applied (by brush, spray, or roller), how thickly or in how many coats, and on whether or not some of the base color bled through. There were instances when paint was merely poured on from buckets and smeared into crude patterns with rags. Exposure to sun and weathering quickly and drastically changed the shade. Tanks in the same unit might have different camouflage patterns, or the shades could vary significantly between old vehicles and recently issued replacements.

In desert regions, vehicles were almost always painted in basic solid sand shades. Pattern-painting was sometimes used, in sand, light and red browns, pale greens, stone gray, etc. The British also made use of pale blue and pink, since this blended well into desert haze and dazzling sun glare, pink being particularly effective at sunrise and sunset. (The US generally shunned those particular colors, for cultural reasons.)

One school of thought held that vehicles were better painted in one solid, subdued color rather than in elaborate camouflaging patterns, which used up materials and man-hours. It was also felt that camouflage patterns were too area-specific, and would become less effective as the terrain and seasons changed. At close ranges, camouflage patterns provided little concealment, and the vehicle could easily be identified by shape; at longer ranges the pattern blended into a solid-appearing color anyway. It was also reasoned that moving camouflage-patterned AFVs, especially when seen from the air, appeared more conspicuous than solid-colored vehicles. The fact of the

matter is that the effectiveness of a patterned or solid-painted finish all depended on the range, angle of view, and lighting conditions. One consideration was that painting vehicles with camouflage patterns improved morale due to the assumption that they gave additional protection, whether that was real or imagined. Even a second's delay caused by hesitation on the part of an enemy gunner in identifying a target could make a difference.

While vehicles may have borne elaborate camouflage patterns, these often conflicted with the need for tactical identification. Such markings included conspicuous national identification, in the form of white five-pointed stars for the US and Commonwealth (often within a white circle), the Soviet red star, and the German white-edged black cross (*Balkenkreuz*). Some commanders opted to obscure or delete national symbols for camouflage purposes. Colored symbols, markings, or numbers were used to identify vehicles within a unit and were usually of high-visibility colors. There were also various alpha-numeric codes for vehicle registration and unit identification, as well as parent unit symbols or formation signs; usually small in size, they were often in non-subdued colors.

Unusually thorough and effective camouflaging of fixed installations at Heraklion, Crete, in 1941. These "local cottages" constructed of sandbags in fact house 12in naval guns removed from the beached HMS *York*; they follow the street alignment of the village, and even have low walls around "vegetable gardens." Obviously, the roof would have to be removed before firing, but it was anticipated that enemy warships and landing vessels would only approach by night. (IWM HU2667)

## Fixed installations

Camouflage painting of buildings, fixed installations, concrete fortifications, and large fixed equipment raised different considerations from vehicles and mobile equipment. The problem was that structures and fortifications, which almost never could be actually "hidden," were often painted in colored mottled and banded patterns that did not match the surrounding terrain. The doctrine was that structures simply painted with subdued colors in disruptive patterns would be misleading enough that enemy pilots would not be able to adequately identify targets during their high-speed attack run. In aerial bombing there is a significant "forward throw," and if the pilot waited too long to release the bombs they would be more likely to miss. The same applied when lining up to engage the target with machine guns.

While the disruptive pattern may have delayed identifying the target, it might have been more effective if the installation had been camouflaged to match the colors and profile of vegetation in the vicinity. Sometimes the colors and patterns that were used contrasted so much with the surrounding terrain that, while the type of installation was difficult to determine, it was nonetheless clearly identifiable as a structure – and, since it was camouflaged, presumably a structure of value.

Mersa Matruh, Egypt, May 1940: men of 2nd Bn, Highland Light Infantry stretch a "shrimp net" – probably the 25ft x 12ft size – as a top dressing for the timber, sandbag, sand and rock overhead cover of a weapon position with a ground-level firing slit; this presumably houses a 2-pdr AT gun. The ungarnished netting would at least blur the outlines and soften any color contrasts when seen from the air. (IWM E90)

## Camouflage nets

Camouflage nets (German, *Tarnnetz*; Russian, *kaskirovochaya setka*; Italian, *rete di mimetizzazione*) came into wide use during World War I, and were first used to conceal artillery. Nets were commonly constructed of knotted string mesh typically in 2–3in squares, and referred to as "fish nets." The much smaller "shrimp net" mesh was typically ¼-inch woven or ½-inch or 1-inch knotted, both types being somewhat stretchy. Nets might be square or rectangular; some were designed to be fastened together to form larger nets, since too large a single net was difficult to erect, remove, and stow.

Narrow strips of differently colored burlap (hessian) sacking or "osnaburg," called "garnish" or "scrim," were woven into the netting.[1] Typically, three colors of garnish were intermixed to give a natural, mottled appearance. Strips were threaded in and out of the mesh squares and knotted at both ends. US and British garnish was issued in 100-yard rolls and the strips were generally cut into 5–6ft lengths – longer strips required too much time to weave through.

The much smaller-mesh "shrimp nets" were not garnished, but dyed. The US used solid OD or sand-colored nets, and UK nets had large, rounded green and brown splotches. They were used with AFVs to hang under trees, or above high brush and saplings to thicken overhead cover, or stretched across angular objects to disguise their perceived shape and prevent reflected shine. They could also be used as simple drape nets.

Firms producing fishing nets switched production to camouflage nets, and all countries employed women to hand-garnish them – a time-consuming task. Mostly bare nets were also issued together with bundles of varied garnish, to allow units to finish nets according to their location. Nets were provided in coloration for temperate forests (predominantly greens), fall/summer (browns, light green), and desert (sand and browns).

---

1 Burlap (US) is made from jute or sisal fibers, and is known as hessian in the UK and Germany. Osnaburg is a coarse linen.

The British issued dark green, light green, light earth, and brown garnish. The US issued pre-colored garnish in seven colors to allow matching with local vegetation and soil coloration. The accompanying panel serves as a guide, but colors and percentages could be modified to conform with local coloration, and for the same reason appropriately colored paints might also be sprayed on all or parts of garnished nets.

| US camouflage drape net garnishing color percentages | | |
| --- | --- | --- |
| *Tropical & summer, temperate* | *Winter, temperate* | *Desert or arid areas* |
| 70% dark green | 60% earth brown | 70% sand |
| 15% olive drab | 30% olive drab | 15% earth yellow |
| 10% field drab | 10% earth red | 15% earth red |

It required a considerable quantity of strips to properly garnish a net. A British 35 x 25ft net required nine 100-yard rolls, and a 14 x 14ft net two rolls. A US 36 x 40ft net required 13 to 20 100-yard rolls, representing 30 man-hours of labor to weave it all in. The garnishing of "drape nets" was not woven in uniformly from edge to edge. It was denser in the central one-third – which was given about 80 percent coverage – and then gradually reduced in density out to the edges, where there was perhaps 10 percent coverage. Overall coverage for the entire net was about 55 percent. The idea was that "drape" nets would be erected over the vehicle, equipment, or structure being concealed on poles of different lengths planted among vegetation, and the edge of the net would drape to the ground at an angle, where it was staked down. This helped eliminate shadows, and the reduced percentage of garnish around the net's periphery allowed it to blend naturally into actual vegetation. In desert areas, nets were more heavily garnished in order to hide the object's shadow beneath the net. The erected net's profile needed to be irregular; this was one of the few instances in the military where precise layout and alignment were discouraged. Nets were most effective if they were integrated or blended into surrounding vegetation, and even more so if cut vegetation was placed on the net; but this needed frequent replacement, and should have been placed in its natural growing position, not simply thrown flat on top in armloads.

This US M4 Sherman tank in Italy appears to have crude pattern-painting, complicated with areas of touch-up painting and spilled oil. The draped "fish net," set up to allow the tank to conduct indirect firing to augment artillery, is garnished as a flat-top net, i.e. with full garnishing to the edges. (Tom Laemlein/Armor Plate Press)

Nets might also be erected as "flat-tops," on poles of the same height and with no draping at the sides; these were often used to conceal dumps of supplies and ammunition. They needed to be erected parallel to the ground (i.e., on a hillside they were to be at the same angle as the slope). They were more effective if at least 2ft headroom was left above the concealed object, the net was fully garnished to the edges, and the edges extended beyond the object for a distance equivalent to twice the net's height. In an area of brush and uniformly high saplings, for instance, a flat-top should have been the same height as them, since it would be conspicuous if either higher or lower.

Nets had to be arranged to accommodate whatever was being concealed. Vehicles, crew-served weapons, and other mobile equipment had to be able to be moved out of the position without time being wasted in removing the net. Weapons had to be able to elevate, traverse, and fire without restriction. To ensure effective concealment the net might drape over the field of fire, but could be quickly lifted or parted to allow firing. Some artillery and AA gun nets used a "clamshell" design, which divided and dropped from each side of a gun barrel at the pull of a quick-release cord.

The vehicle or object under the net should be positioned at an angle so it would not be parallel to the net's edges, to diminish uniformity of appearance. Nets might be partly unrolled and spread to cover a portion of a vehicle when moving. On AFVs, the turret or main gun had to be able to traverse and elevate, but occasionally pieces of netting were secured to turrets and gun barrels. Nets were provided with canvas covers to protect them from snagging and soaking up water while carried on vehicles; they also needed to be dried before storing, to prevent rotting and mildew.

A Soviet AFV commander searches for enemy activity. His vehicle is covered by one common type of Red Army camouflage net, using small patches of attached green fabric as garnish – here far too sparse to be effective, but larger patches were also used. (From the fonds of the RGAKFD in Krasnogorsk via Stavka)

### US ARTILLERY POSITION WITH FLAT-TOP CAMOUFLAGE NET

This cutaway view (**note red lines**) shows a typical net set No.2 concealing a 105mm M2A1 howitzer; it was also issued for the 155mm howitzer and 4.5in gun. The set comprised a 29 x 29ft net, and three 14 x 29ft extension nets rigged one on either side and one to the left or right rear. A flat-top arrangement ensured adequate coverage of the gun, equipment, ammunition, and crew trenches; one or more of the extensions might be angled down to the ground, but this reduced the working space for the crew. The nets came with 18x 10ft poles, wire suspension frames (taut wires strung between the poles), guy lines with turnbuckles, 30 stakes, a 12lb sledgehammer, and two carrying bags. The main net was split for 14ft from the front edge to the center, allowing it to be opened by means of a quick-release latch for higher elevation of the gun. This net is garnished in temperate summer or tropical coloration, the main section thickly, and the extensions more thickly at the edge adjoining the central net than on their outer edges. This crew have been diligent in keeping ammunition, empty shell cases, ammunition boxes, gun equipment, and their personal gear under cover. To hide muzzle-blast burns, ahead of the position chicken wire has been stretched on foot-high stakes and would be covered with brush (removed here for clarity). Ideally the position would be emplaced adjacent to trees, brush, hedges, walls, or any other feature that would shadow it and help it blend in visually (though the tan-colored burlap sandbags used by most armies often matched poorly with the terrain and vegetation). The gun itself is painted OD with a light green disruptive pattern, and light green counter-shading under the barrel and recoil cylinder.

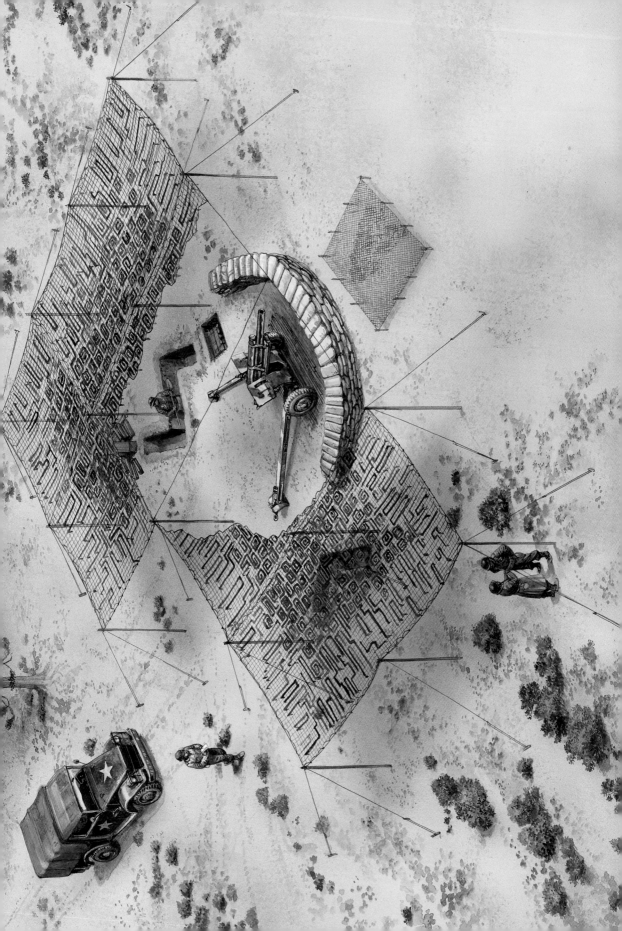

## Wintertime use

Nets were not recommended in snow: they required extensive maintenance, could not bear heavy snow loads, and became wet and difficult to handle; garnishing got wrinkled, lost coverage, increased the texture, and darkened tone values. It was best to remove nets during heavy snow and sleet storms. During thaw periods they could be used with mostly white garnishing, along with mottled gray, black, and olive drab/dark green. Such nets were erected near shadow-casting trees, brush, drifts, outcroppings, etc. White spray paint was sometimes used. However, white garnishing was issued by the Anglo-Canadian 21st Army Group in Europe in the winter of 1944/45. Supplied in 100-yard rolls 3in wide, it was used for garnishing nets, wire netting, and helmets, wrapping gun barrels and small arms, and by snipers.

Snow might adhere to regular colored nets if they were dragged though it, but they were heavy, and might be damaged by snagging on below-snow obstructions. The draped edges on the ground should have had snow thrown over them to distort the outline. Only wooden stakes were used, as metal stakes conducted heat from the sun and thawed themselves free.

The author once helped erect a large World War II-style net, before the new lightweight plastic nets became widely available. It was much heavier than expected, smelled strongly musty and of fabric dye, and caught on every twig and every projection on the vehicle being concealed. Erection of the poles was exasperating, as they had to stand at odd angles, and often fell over before all the edges were staked down. Stakes had to be pulled up and hammered in again while the poles were adjusted, as there was too much tension on some sides of the draped net. The job took almost two hours. Taking it down was not much easier; again, it snagged on everything, and in the meantime it had rained, which made the net about three times heavier. Rolling it up picked up twigs and weeds. It was so heavy that the detail – also thoroughly soaked, just by handling the net – needed extra help to load it into the truck. The next day it was laid out; an hour was spent picking out all the twigs and weeds, and it took two days to dry. It is small wonder that more use of nets was not seen during the war.

Besides camouflaging objects, nets had other uses. Even if the enemy could see the position, the erected net prevented them from determining, for example, what type of artillery piece was being hidden, if the gun was going into action as the crew's activity could not be seen, or determining if there was actually a gun or a decoy under the net. (Of course, the enemy might simply decide that if something was worth erecting a net over, it was worth firing on.) In warm/hot weather and when there was no shade available as in the desert, nets provided welcome shade to gun crews or whoever was sheltered.

The US used four sizes of "net, camouflage, twine, fabric garnished" for specific items of equipment; two or more nets could be fastened together for larger equipment and structures:

15 x 15ft: machine guns, mortars
22 x 22ft: jeep & trailer
29 x 29ft: ¾-ton trucks, trailers, AT guns, light howitzers, scout cars
36 x 44ft: 1½-ton & larger trucks, artillery, tanks, halftracks, other AFVs

American "nets, camouflage, cotton, shrimp" were made in the same sizes as the above twine nets, except that there was a 45 x 45ft size for tanks and self-propelled howitzers, and no 15 x 15ft. Shrimp nets were intended for the

same types of vehicles and equipment as fish nets. The 15 x 15ft fabric-garnished net used lighter string than larger nets, making it compact, lighter, and easier to handle. For this reason it was popular, and two or more could be fastened together; it was not issued with poles, only four stakes.

The US had three special net sets for artillery, which were rigged as "flat-tops" supported by wires rigged as framing on poles. They were accompanied by poles, frame support wires, quick-releases, guy lines, stakes, and carrying cases. Set No.2 was for 105mm and 155mm howitzers and 4.5in guns. It consisted of a 29 x 29ft and three 14 x 29ft extension nets. The No.5 set was for 155mm guns and 8in howitzers, and had one 29 x 29ft and six 14 x 29ft nets. The No.8 set was for 8in guns and 240mm howitzers; it had one 36 x 44ft and two each 17 x 35ft and 29 x 29ft nets.

The standard British garnished "fish nets" were available in five sizes. There were also extension nets available for enlarging artillery nets:

14 x 7ft: 2-pdr AT guns (for screening, not overhead)
14 x 14ft: Bren & Vickers guns, 2in mortars, motor cars, artillery OPs
25 x 14ft: 3in mortars
29 x 29ft: light artillery, AT guns (plus 29 x 14ft extensions)
35 x 35ft: medium & heavy artillery (plus 35 x 17ft extensions)

British "shrimp nets" in five sizes with finer mesh were used over AFVs and other vehicles:

25 x 12ft: 2-pdr AT guns
35 x 15ft: Infantry & Cruiser tanks, scout cars
25 x 12ft: Light tanks, armored cars, Bren gun carriers
14 x 14ft: trucks & lorries up to 30cwt
24 x 24ft: lorries & trailers over 30cwt

Sectionalized poles were issued with nets, but these easily got lost and damaged, and sapling poles were cut and usually retained for further use. The US used mainly wooden stakes, some metal. The British used those,

A US Ninth Air Force mobile air control center in Normandy, mounted on a 2½-ton truck, is covered by a heavily garnished net, dense in the center and sparser to the edges so that it blends into existing foliage. Tree limbs should have been placed over the star, as it shows through the net, and an uncamouflaged truck and courier motorcycles also call attention to the site. However, the "white bumper ends" are actually due to overpainting by a photo censor. (Tom Laemlein/ Armor Plate Press)

as well as metal staples – 8in long, ¼in-diameter prongs, 6in across.

The Soviets used an approximately 4 x 4m (12.5ft) net garnished with cloth strips or colored paper; mesh sizes varied greatly. Any number could be fastened together as necessary. As an alternative to garnishing both the Soviets and the Germans simply spread leafy branches, cut weeds, or straw on bare nets. With the massive expansion of the Red Army and its production priorities, there were few nets to go around; even actual fishing nets were collected from lakes, rivers, and seaports.

The Germans made wide use of camouflage nets in North Africa, to include captured British nets. They were not widely used elsewhere, especially on vehicles, on which natural foliage was commonly used. Nets were mainly used to conceal fortifications, fixed installations, and aircraft.

A US engineer erects a heavily garnished chicken-wire screen to mask vehicle traffic using a main supply route in the forward area from enemy ground observers. There were complaints that issue screens were too lightly garnished to be effective. (US Army)

One standard size was 5 x 5m (16 x 16ft). They used garnished nets, but also nets with angular pieces of colored fabric fastened to them. Garnishing patterns similar to Allied practice were used, as well as less than desirable straight patterns and knotted tufts. The Germans used a variety of canvas tents (*Tarnzelt*), as did all armies. Most used solid brown or green shades, but the Germans used dark field-gray or camouflage pattern-printed in dark green, dark brown, and dark yellow. They also used similar camouflage tarpaulins (*Tarnplanen*).

### CAMOUFLAGE NETS AND PATTERNS

**(1)** The most commonly used fabric garnishing pattern was the "U-shaped," in varied density; the "U"s could be interlocking.

**(2)** The "Greek key" pattern was a tight squared spiral, derived from a decorative border style.

**(3)** The "bow-tie" pattern had short lengths of garnish tied in knots close together, often with the ends hanging.

**(4)** A less common pattern had the strips densely threaded in straight lines or large boxy shapes. This was too regular and conspicuous, unless seen against a consistent background such as sand or snow.

**(5)** The Germans made some early use of irregularly shaped fabric panels fastened to fine mesh nets.

While standards called for relatively dense garnishing, in reality, when the garnishing was done by the troops they found it an extremely monotonous and time-consuming job (the chemical smell of the dye was strong, and fingers got cut or rubbed raw). Inevitably, they became neglectful; often small branches, sprigs of foliage, and weeds were simply spread over nets that were only lightly garnished, if at all.

**(6)** This US 37mm M3A1 AT gun on a Stateside exercise in 1941 is covered by a drooping 15 x 15ft "fish net" without fabric garnish but with foliage sprigs added; the droop improved its effectiveness. An irregularly cut section of sheet metal has been fastened to the top of the gun shield to distort its regular silhouette – a wise, but rare practice. US ammo boxes came in natural wood and were conspicuous if not under cover. While the OD wool trousers were dark brown, the tan 1941 field jacket, web gear and leggings showed up against the OD weapons the crews served and against dark backgrounds. This led to the switch to green OD shades in late 1943.

## Camouflage screens

Screens – which, like nets, had seen widespread use in World War I – mainly protected from ground observation. Owing to their construction and positioning, screens themselves were usually easily detected, but their purpose was simply to prevent the enemy from seeing what was on the other side.

An example is described in a US manual: "Screens for concealing roadblocks may be made of any material – debris, vegetation, or artificial materials variously garnished. The idea is simply to hide the block so that the enemy must make a choice either to run over the screen and risk what is behind it, or to stop and investigate it. If he stops, he is vulnerable to fire. If he tries to run over it, he cannot take advantage of possible weak points in the obstacle." Another example was vertical screens erected to protect bivouacs from enemy patrols, and made of natural materials to blend with the background. Yet another type of screen was placed along portions of roads in view of enemy observers. The enemy knew it was an active road, but the screen denied them observation of the numbers and types of vehicles using it, or the opportunity to acquire individual targets.

Screens could be vertical or sloped, and made from nets, wire mesh (such as chicken wire or galvanized woven hurricane fencing), fabric sheeting, tarpaulins, and any suitable local materials. The latter included tree limbs, boards, and woven grass matting. They were supported by wooden frameworks, poles, stakes, wire, and rope. Hedges, brush lines, tree lines, clumps of trees, and roadside foliage could be incorporated into screens.

One type used by both the Germans and Russians involved pairs of tall poles erected along roads at intervals of perhaps 100 feet. Wire was strung between the paired poles or trees, and panels of garnished netting, wire mesh, or fabric sheets hung vertically between them across the road. The panels themselves might be only 4–6ft high, and were hung high enough to clear vehicles on the road. A fighter pilot making a low-level strafing run down the line of the road was confronted by a succession of screening panels blocking his view of vehicles on the road; he might not even be able to see if there were any, much less target them.

Flat-top screens could be suspended in a similar manner over roads through close forest; these denied aerial visual and photographic observation, and made it very difficult for aircraft traveling at high speed to even locate the road. The screen needed to be level with the treetops; if it was any lower it created a "furrow" appearance through the trees, emphasized by shadows. Such overhead screens obviously required great investment of materials, labor, and time.

## Natural camouflage materials

Natural vegetation is the most effective camouflage material, but care has to be taken in its use. Cut vegetation begins to wilt within 2–4 hours at most; it can be quite noticeable because of differences in color and texture, and the lighter undersides of leaves show up. Camouflaging vegetation must not look out of place. Camouflaging a position with pine saplings on a hillside covered with high grass, weeds, and scattered brush clumps, but no pine stands, simply draws attention. Even fresh-cut saplings and limbs lying horizontally on parapets are conspicuous among vertically growing trees and angled or even horizontal limbs above the ground.

Another mistake is the "trash pile" effect. Piling different types of vegetation or whatever else is available on a position does not "camouflage" it; it may "conceal" it, but the contrast makes it easy to detect. The materials camouflaging

Natural camouflage: men of 1st/4th Bn Essex Regt from 4th Indian Inf Div, dug in near Monte Cassino in spring 1944. The earth and piled-rock parapets of their three-man *sangars* match the lichen-stained cliff face behind them, and roughly resemble the old field walls in the background. The clutter of packs and web equipment left lying in the open underlines the fact that this is a posed photo taken during a quiet period. (IWM NA12894)

a position need to be blended into the surrounding terrain. This applies whether using local vegetation, or rubble, boards, etc, within a destroyed urban area; there must not be an abrupt line defining the edge of the camouflaged area from the somewhat different composition of the surrounding area.

Light is reflected by disturbed soil, especially when it is tamped down. Exposed disturbed soil was a certain giveaway of positions and activity in aerial photos. In black and white photos such soil appeared as vivid pale outlines of positions against dark, undisturbed ground and vegetation, and footpaths and vehicle tracks also appeared white or light gray.

The most effective means of camouflaging the exposed fresh soil around fighting positions was with natural ground cover. This included a layer of topsoil with grass and weeds – essentially, turf – that had reached a point of stability where it would break down no further. It also included dead,

The German crew of this 7.5cm StuG III assault gun perform minor maintenance during a rest halt. It is well camouflaged for cross-country and road movement with foliage, and has leafy branches propped against the bow for additional camouflage while halted. Most of the foliage would be removed when going into action. (Nik Cornish at www.Stavka.org.uk)

matted layers of leaves. Ideally the ground cover would be carefully scooped up in sections and laid aside, not just from where the hole was being dug but also from the ground around it where the spoil dug out would be piled to create the parapet. Once the position was excavated, the sections of ground cover were laid over the parapet and other exposed soil. The second-best option was to cover exposed soil and the bottom of open-topped positions with fallen leaves or conifer needles.

In the frontline care had to be taken when choosing where to gather camouflaging vegetation. It had to be taken from the rear of the line, while bearing in mind that too much cutting could be detected by aerial observation. One or more areas, preferably beneath trees, would be designated from which to cut foliage, or men might be ordered to harvest it over a larger area to make its loss less conspicuous. Care had to be taken to avoid leaving bright, reflective cuts; collectively, the raw stumps of even small recently-cut brush and saplings are conspicuous, and should themselves be concealed by smearing with mud or dirt.

## Expedient camouflage

The first *Afrikakorps* units arriving in Tripoli in early 1941 were not provided with desert camouflage paint; they embarked with dark gray AFVs to keep their deployment from the Continent secret. As an interim measure, oil was rubbed onto the vehicles and sand sprayed on. This had to be repeated frequently, since it quickly wore off. Standard paints were later issued to these units. Other forces used oil or grease for the same purpose, coating it with sand or dirt.

Natural dust and mud adhering to vehicles aided in camouflaging them, and crews were reluctant to wash their vehicles. Mud or clay was intentionally smeared on vehicles in patches and irregular bands or streaks, and was sometimes even specially mixed in buckets to the desired consistency – the Germans did this on the Eastern Front. Mud was used to obscure national markings, especially white stars, when enemy aircraft were a threat. Mud got washed off by rain, and scraped off by driving through vegetation and by the boots of the crews climbing about. Mud usually dried out to a lighter color than wet soil; clay adhered better, and usually dried to the same color as when wet.

A little-used technique was to chop up local foliage, boil it down to a pulp, and smear the resulting paste on vehicles. Since it required picking and chopping large quantities of leaves, vines, and weeds, this was time-consuming – 16x 5-gallon buckets of packed vegetation yielded just 1 gallon of paste. It was easily washed or worn off, and the dried paste might not match live vegetation, though adding cut foliage improved the camouflage effect.

A British dump of 5-gallon petrol cans lightly camouflaged with cut branches, the leaves already wilting. Even with the khaki-green cans lined up along a tree line, they can be detected by a photo interpreter – a uniform row of unnatural squares would attract attention. It would have been better to stack them to appear like a stone wall bordering the field, or in circular domes covered with hay. (Tom Laemlein/Armor Plate Press)

This US M24 Chaffee light tank is reasonably well concealed, being parked hull-down in a drainage ditch with timber wreckage and tree limbs scattered around it. Parking beneath trees gave a measure of concealment even when they had lost their leaves in fall and winter. (Tom Laemlein/ Armor Plate Press)

# INDIVIDUAL CAMOUFLAGE

Camouflage of the individual soldier can be divided under three headings: (1) the normal subdued coloration of uniforms and equipment; (2) special-issue camouflage uniforms and equipment; and (3) camouflage measures undertaken by individuals using natural or locally available materials.

(The following notes on standard-issue uniforms and equipment are, of course, simply the briefest overview; interested readers are recommended to the many other titles in Osprey's Men-at-Arms and Elite series that cover the specifics in far greater detail, broken down by nationality, date and troop types.)

Issue uniforms and equipment for all armies were subdued in color to make them inconspicuous, and appropriate for where they *expected* to fight, that word being significant. Coloration was, of course, suited for their homeland, but most armies conducted operations in regions far from home – and sometimes unanticipated ones.[2] Insignia were often subdued in color, reduced in size, or simply eliminated from combat uniforms.

**America** began the war with uniforms of "khaki" (tan) and "olive drab." US Army "OD" varied widely in color, ranging from light brown to dark green, the specific shades being identified by numbers. Wool uniform items were dark brown, also called OD. The light brown OD uniforms were effective in North Africa, Sicily, and Italy. Gradually darker, greener shades came into use, as better suited for both temperate (European) and tropical regions, and these were in wide use by late 1944.

In Europe very little use was made of camouflage uniforms; in fact, the very few units issued what were termed "frog"-pattern uniforms in Normandy quickly withdrew them, as they were too easily mistaken for the camouflage

---

2 For example, in 1941 sailors of the US Naval Rifle Bn on Bataan attempted to dye their white uniforms khaki using coffee; the result was a yellow tint. From these gaudy uniforms, and the sailors' apparent lack of fear to expose themselves to fire – actually due to their lack of tactical training – the Japanese thought that they were special suicide troops.

US troops conducting patrol training wear the "frog suit" – the herringbone twill reversible camouflage uniform in its five-color pattern. They have draped large-mesh helmet nets over their olive drab hats; arranged as face veils, these provide effective camouflage. Interestingly, these men are armed with Enfield M1917 rifles. (Tom Laemlein/Armor Plate Press)

smocks of German Waffen-SS troops and Fallschirmjäger (paratroopers). There were instances of US paratroopers painting green splotches on their light brown parachutist's uniforms to provide better camouflage in green European woodland; other soldiers, particularly scouts, occasionally did the same.

Boots and other leather gear were russet (reddish) brown. At the beginning of the war the US used dark tan web gear. This was too prominent in forests and jungles, especially when worn over darker colored uniforms, and soldiers occasionally painted green or brown blotches on their belts and pouches. In late 1943 web gear began to be produced in a darker green OD shade, but the old tan gear remained in use throughout the war; tan and green items were often mixed, and sets could be found made with components in both colors. To color tan canvas and webbing to match green OD uniforms, the Quartermaster issued "OQMG No. 3 compound for coloring web equipment." Helmets, entrenching tools, and similar equipment were painted dark OD. In most instances sleeve rank chevrons (conspicuous even though made in subdued colors), officers' collar rank insignia, and colorful unit shoulder patches were removed in the field.

The **British** and other Commonwealth armies used medium brown wool uniforms, of the color referred to in British parlance as "khaki." Like US olive drab, British khaki varied in its exact shade. The sandy-tan color of British tropical uniforms was referred to (by extension from the material traditionally used) as "khaki drill." The KD uniforms worn in North Africa, and later in summertime in Sicily and Italy, were also pre-war standard issue in the Far East. They proved completely unsuitable during the 1941–42 campaigns in the jungles of Malaya and Burma; at first re-dyed green, they were replaced from 1943–44 with dark "jungle green" uniforms.

Boots were black leather. Web gear was made in dark tan, though often scrubbed with compounds that produced many shades between various greens and almost white. From 1944 a new dark green webbing set was produced, but during the war was issued only to troops in the Far East.

US armored infantrymen of the 2nd Armd Div in Normandy wear the M1942 one-piece camouflage suit along with helmets covered with garnished fine-mesh nets. Apart from its similarity to Waffen-SS camouflage, the one-piece suit was inconvenient in that it had to be taken pretty much right off before a man could answer a call of nature. Note the captured Walther pistol holster on the leftmost soldier's belt. (Tom Laemlein/Armor Plate Press)

**BELOW**
The Denison smock was first issued to British airborne forces in 1942, and proved very practical. Made of heavy-duty windproof material lined with wool blanket-cloth, it was camouflaged in broad, ragged streaks of dark green and brown over a mid-green base. It was loosely cut to fit over web equipment during the jump (during which a rear crotch-piece could be pulled forward between the legs and snap-fastened to the lower front), and had four capacious patch pockets. Originally a pullover garment with a zip from the neck, it later unzipped all the way down the front. (IWM)

Little use was made of camouflage clothing, the best-known item being the 1942 Denison smock worn by airborne troops and later some Commandos, which was patterned with broad streaks of green and brown on lighter green. A lightweight two-piece "windproof" suit was also available to selected troops, camouflaged in the same basic pattern. Colorful formation and unit insignia were sometimes removed from battledress in the field, but since they were of small size some or all were often retained – this was a decision for unit commanders. Rank insignia were generally retained in Europe, being of subdued colors; in the Far East all insignia were usually removed.

The **Soviet** Red Army wore rather plain uniforms of olive drab, ranging from medium to dark brown, and light brown or tan in hot southern regions. The standard greatcoat was gray, and tank troops wore black or dark blue suits. Few camouflage uniforms were worn, these being voluminous one-piece coveralls issued to snipers, scouts, and assault engineers. Most were printed in variously colored two-shade patterns of large "cloud" shapes, though one had attached knots of hanging string, and a flecked pattern appeared late in the war. Boots were black. Most personal equipment was originally of medium to dark brown leather, with increasing use of olive drab canvas and webbing as the war progressed. Insignia were limited, and field versions were generally of subdued colors, though troops sometimes wore decorations in combat.

The German Army and Waffen-SS used "field gray" uniforms, a medium grayish-green, but shades varied. In summertime from the mid-war onward, lightweight uniforms in a paler "reed green" (a light dusty green shade) were commonly seen. In North Africa and southern Europe light olive green tropical uniforms were issued, but Luftwaffe troops had their own version in tan cloth. Panzer troops wore specially cut black uniforms; since these were conspicuous, assault gun crews, who often had to dismount to reconnoiter routes and positions, were issued field gray versions of the same uniform.

The Army made very limited use of camouflage uniforms. The principal camouflage item was the general-issue 1931 shelter-quarter (*Zeltbahn*), with a light multi-colored "splinter pattern" (*Splittermuster*) on one side and a darker version on the other. The same angular pattern, and a later, softer-edged "marsh pattern," were used for limited issues of combat smocks and helmet covers from spring 1942 onward, and for reversible camouflage/white padded winter uniforms that became more widely available in 1943/44 (see below). In Italy some use was made of uniforms locally fabricated from Italian Army camouflage fabric; since 1929 Italy had been a pioneer in the use of camouflage material for shelter-quarters. Some officers had camouflage uniforms custom made. Luftwaffe paratroopers were issued long jump-smocks and helmet covers in a similar but not identical "splinter" pattern. The Waffen-SS had pioneered camouflage smocks and helmet covers in distinctive spotted patterns in 1937, and subsequently made wide use of a perplexing variety of spring/summer and fall/winter patterns and colors; they also issued some camouflage field caps, and in 1944 introduced a complete tunic-and-trousers camouflage uniform.

Boots were black. Leather gear was generally black; canvas and web items might be field gray, reed green, drab brown, or tan, and from 1943 equipment could be found in many non-standard colors. The Luftwaffe Fallschirmjäger

Two German riflemen wearing their camouflage shelter-quarters as smocks; this is an early pre-war version of the "splinter pattern" camouflage scheme. They have streaked their faces with charcoal, and have used rubber bands to attach too much bracken and weeds to their helmets; these excessive "antlers" (*Geweihe*) will be conspicuous when they move from cover to cover. (Nik Cornish at www.Stavka.org.uk)

**C**

## CAMOUFLAGE UNIFORMS: PRISONER COLLECTION POINT, NORMANDY, 1944

**(1)** This soldier of the US 2nd Armored Division wears the two-piece herringbone twill camouflage uniform, known like its one-piece predecessor as the "frog suit." This was issued to elements of the 41st Armd Inf Regt and 17th Armd Engr Bn, as well as to some troops of the 2nd and 30th Inf Divs; it was withdrawn within two months due to its dangerous similarity to German camouflage clothing, particularly in dappled sunlight beneath trees (though some individuals wore it for longer). It was reversible, with the inside printed in four shades of tan and brown. Troops generally had helmet nets with burlap garnishing (see Plate E2).

**(2)** A British paratrooper of 6th Airborne Division wears the Denison smock, the first and best-known camouflage garment issued by the British Army. Basically the same camouflage pattern was also used for lighter-weight, hooded "windproof" smocks and matching trousers produced for anticipated operations in Norway, but used elsewhere by some special forces and snipers. The hooded windproof smock was also issued as an over-jacket to some line infantry

in the last winter of the European war – for example, to the motorized infantry of 7th Armd Div's 131 (Queen's) Brigade.

**(3)** The para is bringing in two captured Waffen-SS soldiers. This veteran wears a helmet cover and smock in one of the many variations of colors and spotted patterns produced before and during the war, and often seen mixed within the same units.

**(4)** This teenage SS-Mann, perhaps from 12. SS-Pz Div *"Hitlerjugend,"* has the 1944 camouflage uniform consisting of a four-pocket tunic and trousers in what is commonly called *Erbsenmuster* or "peas pattern," with a matching cap.

**(5)** The wounded Luftwaffe paratrooper of Fallschirmjäger Regt 6 has the distinctive helmet cover and jump-smock of his arm of service, in the Luftwaffe version of "splinter pattern" introduced from 1941; this differed slightly from the Army's 1931 pattern used for the general-issue shelter quarter, on which he is lying. (Camouflage trousers were not provided with either the Waffen-SS or Fallschirmjäger smocks.) The different patterns of camouflage cloth developed by the Army, Luftwaffe, and Waffen-SS were a wasteful duplication encouraged by the "turf wars" between the services.

The Waffen-SS crew of an MG34 squad light machine gun early in the war. Factory-made camouflage smocks and helmet covers were exclusive to the Waffen-SS until 1942. They were carefully designed, and little expense was spared in their manufacture; the covers had spring-hooks to engage with the helmet rim, the smocks had elasticated cuffs with a "frill" to cover the hands, and both items eventually had integral loops for attaching foliage to the helmet and shoulders.

were unique in using some web gear manufactured in camouflage patterns, namely ammunition bandoliers and grenade pouches. The Germans retained a degree of the Prussian splendor in their rather elaborate uniform insignia. Dull gray was substituted for white and silver elements, and shoulder straps of rank were sometimes worn face down or fitted with cloth covers, but regardless of war economy and visibility they retained branch-of-service color piping. It was common for badges and awards to be worn on the tunic in the field – they were sometimes seen even on camouflage clothing, despite the production of special subdued insignia for that purpose.

### "Over-white" snow camouflage clothing

Although troops often had to improvise early in the war, loose-fitting white snow-camouflage garments were subsequently issued by all armies. These were often pioneered by or exclusive to specialist troops such as mountain, ski, and commando units, but in many cases regular infantry and other frontline troops were also issued them.

The Soviets already made wide use of one-piece over-white coats or two-piece suits in the Russian winter, and from winter 1941/42 the Germans were obliged to copy them. Before factory-made garments became available there were instances of German units contracting local Russian women to fabricate over-whites. It was more common, however, for soldiers to improvise their own helmet covers, snow capes and smocks from bed linen. Strips torn from sheets were also wrapped around weapon barrels and other equipment.

Such garments were typically of thin cotton or linen and offered no insulation, being intended purely for camouflage. Over-whites were

Waffen-SS junior officers wearing camouflage smocks relax in front of their *Wohnbunker* (living bunker) in a Russian forest. The bunker's entrance is shielded by shelter-quarters in Waffen-SS camouflage pattern rigged so as to conceal from the air the shadow caused by the door. (Nik Cornish at www.Stavka.org.uk)

designed for web gear to be worn beneath them, and had slits for access to ammunition pouches and uniform pockets. However, web gear was often worn on the outside for convenient access, and this actually enhanced camouflage in areas with vegetation or during thaw conditions. Over-white mittens, pack covers and helmet covers were also used by all armies. Skis, ski poles, snowshoes, and other equipment habitually used in the snow were painted white.

Distinct from camouflage over-whites, from 1942 the Germans produced thickly insulated two-piece winter suits designed to both protect and conceal the wearers. Featuring hooded anoraks or parkas, these popular garments were produced by both the Army and the Waffen-SS. They were made to be worn reversibly, with either gray or camouflage pattern on one side and white on the other.

With prolonged wear, over-whites and other white clothing become dirty and conspicuous. In open areas of snow, faces, gloves, boots, packs, web gear, and weapons could show up, negating snow camouflage; white face masks were sometimes issued. Another problem was friend-or-foe identification. The Germans and Russians sometimes used colored cloth bands on one or both sleeves for close-range recognition; the "color of the day" could be changed regularly, but this was not widely practiced.

German Army helmet cover and smock in "splinter pattern" camouflage, as produced from 1942. These were more simply made than the Waffen-SS equivalents, and never became general issue.

US troops, wearing locally fabricated linen snow capes and helmet covers in winter 1944/45, pull a sled with a wounded man. Such garments quickly became soiled, but in snow-covered urban areas this actually helped them to blend in. (Tom Laemlein/Armor Plate Press)

## Steel helmets

The helmets used by the US, British Commonwealth, USSR, and Germany all left the factory finished in broadly similar dark olive drab or green colors. German helmets varied in shade depending on the manufacturer, and might be painted in matt or semi-matt finish. When wet, no matter what the paint finish, steel helmets glisten in the light, and especially at night if there is a moon or starlight or nearby artificial illumination. Sometimes mud was smeared on helmets to prevent reflections and for camouflage. While camouflage pattern-painted helmets existed, these were rarely seen. American helmets often had finely crumbled cork mixed into the paint to make them less reflective, and the British and Germans sometimes used sand in the same way, especially in North Africa. The US used M5 liquid vesicant detector paint (which turned red if in contact with liquid mustard gas agent) to apply disruptive patterns on helmets, this being a lighter shade than the factory-finish olive drab.

In North Africa, German and British Commonwealth forces often painted helmets sand-color. During winter snows helmets were often whitewashed, or furnished with improvised white cloth covers; the Germans sometimes pasted on white paper. Troops of all armies used various forms of helmet covers, both issue and expedient, made up from usually tan-colored sandbag fabric or burlap feed sacks. Such covers eliminated reflections,

German troops show off their new two-piece hooded over-white suits, and long mitten gauntlets, outside a bunker on the Eastern Front in winter 1942/43.

softened the helmet's familiar silhouette, and helped muffle the noise when foliage struck helmets; they also aided the attachment of foliage for camouflage, though this need was more usually filled by the issue of string helmet nets.

The US made use of large-mesh nets from 1943, occasionally with garnishing attached. In 1944 a much smaller mesh of heavier, "stretchy" string was issued, along with an elastic neoprene band that passed around the lower portion of the crown. This was intended to hold the net so that it could hang free over the face, rather than being fixed by being tucked up between the helmet liner and steel shell. The British used small to medium-mesh nets from early in the war; in 1939–40 some units of the British Expeditionary Force in France made up neat tan hessian covers with loops for inserting vegetation, and individuals and units used sandbag fabric for more roughly-made covers throughout the war.

In the German Waffen-SS, camouflage-pattern fabric helmet covers with foliage-attachment loops were general issue, but the Army used a much wider variety of helmet coverings, since they were poorly supplied with factory-made types. It was 1942 before camouflage-pattern covers reversible to white became available, along with twine mesh nets with fixing hooks, and both seem always to have been in short supply. A popular practice was to improvise camouflage-holding bands by cutting narrow rubber rings from old vehicle tire inner tubes. Another widespread method used the removable canvas shoulder sling provided with, but seldom needed for, the issue

## GERMAN SNOW CAMOUFLAGE

**D**

Both Russian and (more gradually) German troops became adept at snow camouflage, developing their own techniques and copying each other. The position being constructed here (which would actually be less cramped than is dictated by the limits of the page) has crawl trenches and fighting positions dug in the snow, floored with cut saplings and fir-tree trimmings, and overlaid with mats of woven willow branches or wire mesh. These were covered with brush or straw, or with layers of paper that had been wetted and allowed to freeze solid. This layer would, in its turn, be covered with snow, but was not effectively camouflaged until fresh snow had fallen. The mats could be raised slightly at an edge for observation or firing. At left, ammo crates are stacked and lightly covered with snow, with fir saplings placed among them; the saplings mark the location, while they and their shadows help hide the disturbed snow.

### Clothing

Experiments with the standard German off-white denim drill uniform were a failure, since it was too close-fitting be worn over insulating layers of clothing. Units or depots often fabricated snow-camouflage clothing using local resources. The types illustrated were all seen during the first two winters

in Russia. Helmets were usually whitewashed, either solid or in dappled pattern, but reversible white/camouflage covers were occasionally seen.

**(1)** The simplest expedient was a bed sheet taken from a local home. Draped over both head and torso, it was secured with a rubber band around the helmet and a cord round the waist.

**(2)** The snow shirt was a locally made pullover item hanging to the knees; the improvised helmet cover hid the back of the neck and gave some wind protection.

**(3)** The loose-fitting two-piece snow suit had a front-buttoning, unlined, hooded parka and baggy trousers, for wear over winter clothing. Black and red cloth armbands were issued for buttoning to one or both sleeves, giving eight possible variations that could be changed periodically, like passwords.

**(4)** Like the two-piece, one-piece snow suits were a factory-produced item.

**(5)** Another issue garment was a loose-fitting smock, reversible from white to splinter-pattern camouflage.

**(6)** Going on sentry duty, this soldier wears a one-piece hooded overgarment cut like a coat, heavy gloves, and big straw overboots to insulate his feet.

German Army infantrymen in 1943/44 clothed in the two-piece, reversible, hooded, insulated winter suit issued from winter 1942/43. The white side reversed to either gray or, as here, the "splinter" camouflage pattern. Combining concealment with warmth, this suit was a popular item. (Nik Cornish at www.Stavka.org.uk)

haversack or "bread bag"; this could be passed around the helmet and over its crown from side to side, and clipped to the rim on each side with its dog-lead end hooks. Chicken wire might be shaped roughly to the helmet and the edges turned up under the rim. Covers were improvised from burlap and with camouflage cloth from worn-out shelter-quarters, and there were instances of British and US helmet nets being used.

When attaching foliage to helmets, only just enough leafy twigs and weeds should be used to break up the silhouette, to include a little protruding along the lower rim. It should be changed when it wilts and discolors, or when the soldier moves to an area with noticeably different ground vegetation. It is a mistake to attach too much vegetation, especially if it extends much above the helmet, since even small head movements will cause these "plumes" to wave and attract attention. Too much foliage also catches on other vegetation when moving. For all these reasons, substituting strips of cloth garnish woven in and out of the netting usually provided a better solution; in the British Commonwealth forces such "scrim" was standard issue, and soldiers were taught its correct use.

## Individual equipment

Belts, suspender yokes, pouches, canteen and gasmask carriers, entrenching tools, bayonet scabbards, backpacks, haversacks, and many other items were of subdued colors, but usually contrasting with that of the uniform, with metal fittings usually stained black or in dulled brass. This actually helped camouflage soldiers: the slight variations in color and texture, and the shadows and irregularities created on the soldier's body, distorted familiar forms. It was rare, but web gear was sometimes painted with green or brown splotches or streaked with charcoal. It was sometimes whitewashed, but usually not, as its darker shade usefully broke up the shape of solid over-white suits when among trees and other vegetation.

Apart from the appearance, it was essential for patrol members to "silence" their gear and weapons. Metal-on-metal contact was avoided by proper equipment positioning, and inserting cloth items as padding between metal items in packs; socks were useful for this, and soldiers often carried extras.

Ration cans also had to be padded, and metal buckles and snaphooks might be taped. Ammunition was packed so that it would not rattle; some types of magazines – especially drums – tended to rattle because of the loose seating of the cartridges. Canteens were initially full to prevent audible sloshing. Boots could not creak, and loose items in pockets had to be wrapped or removed.

Foliage was occasionally tucked into the belts and suspenders around the body, but this was usually more trouble than it was worth (see comments above on the drawbacks of over-enthusiastic helmet camouflage). If just enough was attached to distort the soldier's form, it could be used effectively in the short term when infiltrating close to enemy positions. It could also be useful if enemy aircraft flew over; the key here was for moving soldiers to immediately halt, crouch (prone bodies are more easily identified from the air), and resist exposing their pale faces by looking up at the aircraft, even after it had passed.

British troops received as general issue a 3ft x 3ft 6in "veil" of cotton "shrimp net" dyed in a camouflage pattern of green and brown blotches. This was a multipurpose item, for draping over the helmet and face, or the pack and shoulders when prone. Up to 1941 the Russians had also issued a small net to individual infantrymen, about 2.5 x 4.5ft (0.76 x 1.37m). Garnished with local vegetation, it could cover part of the soldier and his foxhole's parapet, and could also be draped over his helmet, shoulders, and pack for camouflage while on the move. However, issue ceased after the German invasion. The Russians used other camouflage gear for which only brief descriptions are available from German sources:

> "*Camouflage screen for rifleman* This consists of a [fan-like] wire contraption divided into several pieces, covered with [garnish] material. In it is a hole through which the rifle can protrude. It represents a bush, and is in use in three different colors. It can be folded up and carried on the person in a bag. The rifleman lies in such a position behind the screen that his body is fully hidden. In attacking he can move forward in a crouch and push the screen in front of him. The screen is only visible to the naked eye at a distance of 150–200 paces.
>
> "*Camouflage cover for machine gun* The cover consists of colored fabric in which tufts of colored matting are woven. When moving forward, the cover will not be taken off. The machine gun with this cover can only be recognized when within about 100m.
>
> "*Camouflage fringe* This consists of a band about 3m long, from which grass-colored matting is hung. On the ends are hooks for attaching the fringe on the object. The rifleman can fix the fringe on the helmet or shoulders. Five of these fringes are used to camouflage a machine gun, and six for an antitank gun."

German Panzergrenadiers in a deep trench in North Africa, 1942, wearing sand-colored helmet covers neatly sewn from sacking or canvas, probably at unit level. Their tropical uniforms are olive green; with sun-bleaching and washing the color faded considerably, and some troops, wishing to appear as *alter Hasen* ("old hares" – combat veterans) deliberately bleached their uniforms paler with *Losantin* anti-mustard gas tablets (chlorine bleach). Copying originally from Italian practice in this theater, the Germans became adept at constructing deep, narrow trenches without parapets, making them difficult to detect from the air or ground. (IWM HU5604)

Some German units used "string vests" locally made from netting, which covered the front and back of the torso down to the hips. These had head and arm openings, and a matching helmet net, and were to be garnished with vegetation. Such vests proved impractical, since they constantly snagged on foliage. Other German units made sleeveless smocks or tabard-like vests from old shelter-quarters, or from subdued-color cloth hand-painted with disruptive patterns. These practices were common in Normandy. Mosquito head-nets were fine mesh hoods covering the head and shoulders; they had the secondary benefit of effectively concealing helmet outlines and faces, and were useful to snipers. German snipers also made simple face masks from camouflage *Zeltbahn* fabric, to supplement issue veils made of curtains of string tassels attached to helmets.

**E**

## HELMET CAMOUFLAGE

The most common way for a soldier to camouflage himself was to alter the appearance of his helmet – to cut reflected glare, distort its familiar silhouette, and provide a means to attach natural or manmade garnish. While most armies issued helmets factory-finished in drab-colored matt paint, sometimes with an admixture of crumbled cork or sand, an uncovered and uncamouflaged helmet was still all too recognizable on the battlefield.

**(1)** The US Army at first used a large-mesh net for the M1 helmet. The net was draped over the helmet's steel shell and tucked up inside, held firm when the fiber liner was replaced.

**(2)** The Army later adopted a more "stretchy" type in ¼ to ½-inch mesh, with an elastic neoprene band. Painted rank insignia were seldom seen in the field, though simplified vertical and horizontal bar shapes were sometimes painted on the rear by officers and NCOs respectively. Soot was sometimes smeared on the face for night patrols.

**(3)** Individual camouflage painting of helmets was rare, but more common in airborne units, as was the addition of burlap garnishing to the net. The parachutist's first aid packet is attached to the net of this M1C helmet, and Type 1 luminous markers, to aid assembly on a night drop zone, are attached to the sides.

**(4)** The British used both a medium-sized mesh of about 1-inch squares, and this small-mesh net, similar to "shrimp netting"; this might be dyed all green, in green and brown patches, or – in Italy – sandy tan. This Mk II helmet has the "first field dressing" tucked inside the stretchy net. Both types of net were secured by a drawstring tied beneath the brim. Some helmets were given a combination of the wider-mesh net worn over a roughly improvised hessian cover.

**(5)** The British Mk III "tortoise" helmet was widely issued in NW Europe from 1944, with priority for units committed to the Normandy landings; it was increasingly seen worn by replacements reaching the front thereafter, though both types continued to be worn side by side. The standard small-mesh net was often torn with larger holes, or had extra lengths of string woven and tied on, to fix hessian "scrim"; the latter was deliberately frayed to soften the outline still further. The shape of the Mk III made it convenient to tuck the field dressing packet under the net above the deeper rear brim.

**(6)** British paras similarly camouflaged their helmets – here the third pattern – with nets, plentiful garnish and lengths of cord. The demands of camouflage usually overrode those of unit morale, and in combat units painted unit flashes on the sides of helmets were seldom seen overseas after 1940, though they were not unknown in North Africa. This unusual example of a helmet flash in Normandy, 1944, is that of the Oxfordshire & Buckinghamshire Light Infantry (dark blue/yellow/dark red/dark blue). D Company of the 2nd Bn Ox & Bucks, led by Maj John Howard, provided the glider troops for the seizure of the vital bridges over the Orne river and canal on the eastern flank of the Allied landing zones in the early hours of D-Day. Since the general-issue camouflage net "veil" was soft to the touch, soldiers' shirts were collarless, and the collars of serge Battledress were scratchy, many men cut lengths to use as scarves inside opened BD collars.

**(7)** This German M1935 helmet has a crude knotted net over a homemade frame of twisted wire, for holding twigs and foliage (which German soldiers called *Geweihe*, "antlers"). Factory-made nets, ordered into production in August 1942, were made of "hairy" brown twine in varying sizes of mesh, usually quite large; they came with four zinc wire hooks to engage the helmet rim, but these very often got detached, and soldiers tied the nets on as best they could. The national and Army decals originally applied to the right and left sides of the helmet were ordered discontinued in March 1940 and August 1943, respectively, but photos show that individuals might continue to wear them.

**(8)** German M42 helmet fitted with a chicken-wire crown for securing foliage, and a rubber band cut from a tire inner tube (which was often used alone). The wire often extended down to tuck under the edge, and much larger-mesh fencing wire was sometimes used for these improvised covers.

**(9)** Factory-made fabric covers reversible from "splinter-pattern" camouflage to plain off-white were produced from 1942, with loops for attaching foliage and a tunnel for tightening a drawstring under the rim. An early variant was reversible from "mouse-gray" to white, and from 1943 examples also appeared in the softer-edged "marsh-pattern" camouflage. Such covers were never available in large numbers, and veterans have suggested that when they did arrive units gave priority to high-risk personnel – unit leaders, and the crews of machine guns, mortars and AT guns. Many other covers were made individually or at unit level from old *Zeltbahn* cloth, sacking, canvas, or Italian camouflage fabric.

## Small arms

These were not often camouflaged. Most were made of black or near-black gunmetal with wooden stocks and grips, and leather or web slings. It was their shape that tended to make them conspicuous, and only very rarely were they painted, although the Germans occasionally whitewashed weapons. All armies created such a fetish about the cleaning and maintenance of weapons that the idea of painting them was instinctively repugnant. Attaching vegetation was usually impractical, but snipers often wrapped cloth garnish and/or other materials around their rifle barrels. This had to be done with care: the camouflage could not interfere with loading, changing magazines or belts, cocking, clearing, movement of external operating parts like the bolt or cocking handle, or the use and adjustment of sights.

## Face camouflage

Natural skin oils make the face glisten, especially the forehead, nose, cheekbones, and jaw line, so for night patrols and raids soldiers often "blackened" their faces, ears, necks, and the backs of their hands and wrists. Snipers sometimes followed this practice in daylight too, and it was virtually a trademark of Commandos, Rangers, and other special-forces soldiers. The combined US/Canadian 1st Special Service Force was said to be known to the Germans as the "Black Devils," the name originating at Anzio when blackened-face Forcemen aggressively conducted raids and harassing patrols within German lines.

The most common source of face-blacking was wine and beer bottle corks (said to be more effective if the contents of the bottle was drunk first…). The cork's end was burnt with a match, candle, or lighter, allowed to cool for a

Field Marshal Rommel and staff officers inspect the crew of a hybrid 10.5cm assault gun mounted on a French Hotchkiss tank chassis in Normandy. The gun crew wear unit-made camouflage vests – simple burlap pullover items, hand-painted in green. Such garments were referred to as *Messgewarde* or "vestments." (Nik Cornish at www.Stavka.org. uk)

few seconds, and rubbed on the face; the black deposit adhered fairly well. Charcoal or soot from fireplaces or stoves was also effective, but when a man sweated the powdery material rubbed off easily. Black or brown boot polish was sometimes used, but was uncomfortably oily or waxy and difficult to clean off. Bootblack was also *too* black, making it conspicuous, and it glistened even when dry. Mud was occasionally used, but this too was uncomfortable, sweated or rubbed off easily, and might contain harmful bacteria.

A mistake with face-blacking was to overdo it; painting the face uniformly solid black was too conspicuous if there was any ambient light at all. It was better to apply the blacking in streaks, irregular bands, or dabbed patches. Another mistake was to apply blacking heavily, but not around the eyes and mouth; this produced an effect reminiscent of the stereotyped caricature of a negro, familiar in those unenlightened days from theatrical so-called "minstrel shows." Because the lips and eyeballs could not be blackened, men were advised to keep their mouths tightly closed and eyes half-closed when in close proximity to the enemy.

In 1944 the US issued stick-form camouflage face paints. These were small tinplate tubes with caps on both ends, containing hard paste sticks colored light green at one end and "loam" (very dark green) at the other; for desert areas, sand and light green; or for snow regions, white and loam. These saw little use before the war's end.

A British para manning a Projector, Infantry, Anti-Tank Mk I (PIAT), wearing a somewhat tattered small-mesh helmet net with the remnants of garnishing. He has also draped a general-issue "veil" over his shoulders and back; this soft cotton "shrimp net" was camouflage-dyed in large green and brown rounded blotches. (IWM)

## Individual concealment

Soldiers were taught to move cross-country using any available concealment. They also learned various techniques that helped them to remain inconspicuous and minimize their exposure. Simple rules were applied to individual concealment when either static or moving:

*Day concealment when static:*
- When not observing, keep as close to the ground as possible.
- Keep still until movement is necessary.
- Whenever possible observe lying down, or from whatever position will expose you the least.
- Keep off the skyline.
- Avoid single or small clumps of trees and bushes as they stand out and attract enemy fire.
- Avoid positions at easily described points, such as fence corners, angles in walls, or anywhere else that is distinctive and allows an enemy observer to describe the point to a weapon crew.
- If moving from one observation position to another, first move out of the enemy's line of sight and then move to another position.

Soldiers of the US 63rd Inf Div prepare for a night patrol toward the Siegfried Line. They are passing around a plate of soot scraped from a kitchen stove to blacken their faces. Charcoal and burnt cork were also popular for this purpose. (Tom Laemlein/Armor Plate Press)

*Day movement:*
- When in the open, lie motionless with your body stretched flat.
- To observe, lift your head slowly and steadily. Make no abrupt or quick movements.
- Before relocating, note positions the enemy might occupy and plan your route to avoid observation from those points.
- Select your route in advance before moving from one position to another.
- Use any available concealment when moving, no matter how insignificant.
- Cross over skylines where hidden by vegetation, or by low-crawling.
- Remain in shadows as much as possible.
- Ensure vegetation you are passing through is moved or shaken as little as possible.
- Be aware that in the morning hours you may leave a distinctive trail through dew-covered vegetation. The same applies to snow and frost-covered ground.
- Use battlefield sounds and weather sounds (rain, wind) to cover the sound of your movement.
- Know where you are at all times, and do not become lost or confused as to the direction of your own troops.
- Be aware that a static enemy may be encountered anywhere, no matter how unlikely, and moving from any direction – to include behind you, especially if you are beyond your own lines.

*Night movement:*

- Keep off skylines, and avoid getting silhouetted against light backgrounds.
- Follow tree and vegetation lines and other terrain features. Do not follow a route across open ground just because it is dark.
- Remain in shadows as much as possible. Moonlight can cause you to cast a shadow.
- Maintain absolute light and noise discipline.
- Move slowly, stepping high to avoid brushing low foliage. Feel with the toe for twigs, dry leaves, gravel, etc, before putting your foot down.
- Take advantage of background noises (wind, rain, vehicles, battlefield noises) to cover your movement.
- If you hear the pop of a flare being launched, hit the ground and freeze. If surprised by a flare, freeze immediately. Never look at a flare, as it causes lengthy night blindness.

An unofficial phrase was "good patrolling weather," an ill-defined term that any infantryman will nevertheless understand. It can be described as cool, showery weather in which the patrol becomes neither overheated, nor soaked and too cold; it is chilly and wet enough to make bored static sentries try to shelter from the drizzle, thus reducing their alertness. While the patrol may be damp, their discomfort is offset by the quieter movement allowed by the rain, wet vegetation and ground cover. Mist or fog may accompany these conditions, further limiting enemy visibility.

## Light discipline

At dusk and after dark this was obviously essential. Any source of light on a battlefield could let an enemy know where troops were located, and might draw fire. In an era when the majority of troops smoked and regarded tobacco as relaxing, there was a strong temptation to smoke when on boring sentry duty. The flare of a match or lighter could be seen for miles, and the glowing end of a lit cigarette for hundreds of yards. Even if a soldier stayed ducked down in his position, the smell of tobacco could still alert a questing enemy patrol.

Flashlights (torches) and candles used to study maps at night had to be shielded. A poncho, shelter-quarter, blanket, raincoat, or a couple of jackets had to be draped over the men studying a map or writing a message, and it was best to do this among dense vegetation or in low ground. Kerosene, gasoline, oil and charcoal stoves, lanterns, candles, and makeshift "trench lights" inside bunkers and shelters all had to be shielded. Firing ports and entrances were covered, and double-blackout curtains or doors were installed in entrances. Cooking/warming fires could not be used or were tightly controlled in the frontlines. Even small fires using dry hardwoods and avoiding green, sappy, rotten, or wet wood would still create smoke and odor. Fires beneath trees, while not obvious to those around them, caused treetops and the underside of leafy limbs to glow.

Vehicles were fitted with hooded or masked driving lights that provided just enough illumination to make out the road immediately ahead of the vehicle. This of course required a very low speed, and it was wise to use a walking guide so as to avoid obstacles and sleeping soldiers.

One form of light discipline was preventing reflections from binoculars and optical weapon sights. The latter were often fitted with front lens shields, and binoculars could be similarly shielded by placed the cupped hands so that they extended beyond the front lens. If observing or firing from inside a building, standing back from the window in the room's shadows prevented reflections and helped shield muzzle flashes. When not needed, goggles were often pulled up onto the forehead, helmet, or cap, thus inviting reflections; it was better to pull them down around the neck.

# VEHICLE CAMOUFLAGE

Camouflage of vehicles depended not only on concealing them, but preventing or concealing their tracks, eliminating reflections, distorting their shapes and shadows, and painting them in appropriate colors. ("Vehicles" here refers equally to any other mobile equipment or large weapons.)

## Siting

Regardless of how well camouflaged a vehicle might be, if it was poorly sited it could be detected. Positioning within shadows was useful; in the northern hemisphere, the north side of an object higher than the vehicle was the best side to park on. The east and west sides were dangerous for the first and second halves of the day, respectively, but even if the object casting the shadow was lower than the vehicle it might help hide it. The use of nets or placed vegetation would help, as would siting vehicles on dark, rough terrain.

Too many vehicles hidden in a relatively small area might draw attention, and dispersal was important. Vehicles and crew-served weapon positions anyway had to be dispersed for protection from artillery and air attack. There is no set distance for dispersal, although 50ft between vehicles and weapons was a rough rule of thumb to prevent one artillery round from damaging two targets. "Dispersal" (distances separating vehicles/positions within an area or formation) or "interval" (distance been vehicles in a column) depended on visibility (day or night, clear weather or rain, snow, or fog), on terrain, vegetation, and threat, and might be anything from 50 to 300 feet. If threatened by air attack, for example, vehicles traveling on a road would leave long intervals between them, but less so for artillery attack. A key factor was inter-visibility, so that each vehicle, position, etc, could see the others so as to prevent separation or cover gaps.

When a column of vehicles halted in forward areas it was common practice for alternating vehicles to pull off opposite sides of the road; this was called "herringbone-pattern," as they usually pulled off at an angle. However, if roadside trees, hedges, or buildings cast shadows over the road it was better to park there, though ditches, walls, fences, and vegetation might prevent vehicles from clearing the road at such points.

Vehicles should park under the cover of trees, but if these are absent or inadequate they should park to conform to the terrain pattern and not in the open. That means parking parallel to straight lines – road and trail edges, fences, walls, or hedges. In urban areas they should park close to buildings or in alleys. Vehicles could also be parked among previously destroyed vehicles. If traversing cultivated fields, then if possible they drove parallel to plowed furrows and not perpendicular or diagonally to them; if this was impossible then it was best to drive along the margins, parallel to bordering fences, walls, and hedges. Of course, tactical situations often prevented these ideal practices.

The priority for siting weapons was fields of observation and fire. It was too easy to select the "best" position – exactly where the enemy would look and expect them. Even if they were well concealed, the enemy might barrage likely areas as a precaution, or conduct reconnaissance by fire.

In the desert and other barren areas such as the Russian steppes, shadows and tracks often gave away vehicles on the featureless terrain. The lower the vehicle the better, as it cast less shadow. Digging-in a vehicle even partly lowered its profile and made it easier to camouflage with nets, but the amount of effort required was significant, and the large quantities of disturbed and displaced soil also called attention to the site. The use of low ground, gullies, wadis, and clumps of vegetation all helped.

This US reconnaissance unit's jeep and M8 light armored car have parked alongside a fence in order to blend into the terrain pattern, and are well camouflaged against aerial observation using hastily applied local materials in the form of cut saplings and limbs. A deficiency is the jeep's raised windshield, which is likely to reflect glare. (Tom Laemlein/ Armor Plate Press)

This PzKpfw VI Tiger I is finished in three-color camouflage painting over the *Zimmerit* plaster that was applied in order to frustrate Soviet hand-placed magnetic charges; its matt, ridged texture also aided the camouflage effect. When camouflaging vehicles the Germans made much more use of natural foliage, as here, than of nets or tarps. (Nik Cornish at www.Stavka.org.uk)

This US M10A1 tank destroyer has parked amid wreckage next to a French church, and planks have been laid against its side to break up its distinctive profile and features. Tossing any available wreckage and tree limbs against a halted vehicle was standard procedure, being easier and much faster than unrolling a camouflage net. (Tom Laemlein/Armor Plate Press)

## Early German use of camouflage and concealment

In 1939–40 considerable ingenuity was shown in Poland and France in concealing minefields and artillery, but disruptive painting of motor transport and armored vehicles was apparently little practiced. The use of dummy positions appears to have been very common: field guns were concealed in dummy haystacks, AT guns and limbers were disguised as carts (and even driven by soldiers disguised as civilians). On the other hand, parachutes with straw dummies attached and canisters with bogus instructions were dropped to create alarm. There appears, in fact, to have been a frequent offensive use of camouflage to enable all kinds of ruses to be carried out.

 **CAMOUFLAGE CONTRASTS**

There were two main schools of thought about the camouflage-painting of vehicles and other large equipment. Some preferred a single solid color that blended in with most vegetation backgrounds. Others believed that a solid base color overpainted with simple, bold patterns in a contrasting, usually darker shade was more effective.

**(1)** This US M4 Sherman medium tank is painted with a black pattern over an olive drab base. Such schemes were more effective at longer ranges, since a bold contrasting pattern tended to break up the tank's visual outline, and hampered an enemy gunner's estimation of range. At closer ranges it might actually draw attention, but would usually remain reasonably effective if the tank was among shadows or dense vegetation. On this tank the white star national markings on the vertical surfaces have been painted over, and some scraps of camouflage netting have been fastened to the turret.

**(2)** This German PzKpfw V Panther tank demonstrates the opposite approach. From August 1944 AFV production plants were ordered to apply a camouflage pattern over the base color before delivery rather than leaving that task to the receiving units. German forces were now principally on the defensive, with tanks and assault guns typically conducting close-range attacks from concealed positions, so camouflage was designed to conceal them in woodland – it also proved reasonably effective in rubble-strewn urban areas. This "ambush camouflage" (*Hinterhalt zu tarnen*) varied in detail depending upon the manufacturer; here we show a pattern used by Daimler-Benz. The dark yellow base color was spray-painted with irregular olive green and red-brown splotches; a dappled effect was then achieved by spraying small spots of dark yellow on the green and brown areas, and green and/or brown spots on the yellow areas. Note that the road wheels are painted in a single color, and the main gun barrel is not dappled, but has yellow counter-shading along its underside. Neither the conspicuous national cross insignia nor tactical turret numbers are displayed.

The following are comments on the German use of camouflage early in their presence in Libya in 1941:

- They were initially deficient in dispersal in the open desert, making them vulnerable to air and artillery attack, but they learned quickly.
- Some use of drape camouflage nets and locally procured cloth for screens. Vertical screens were used by armored cars in ambush positions. Nets without fabric garnishing were garnished with vegetation only. They also used cut vegetation to conceal vehicles.
- German artillery was positioned among abandoned Italian guns near Capuzzo in July 1941, and was undetected until it opened fire.
- Pairs of spare truck tires were rolled through minefields to lure in British scout cars.
- Much use was made of decoy positions and dummy minefields.
- Fuel and ration dumps were hidden in 18in-deep pits located well away from landmarks, well dispersed, and covered with brush.

A report written by a German infantry battalion commanding officer in North Africa throws interesting light on the difficulties caused by excessive orderliness of mind and lack of practice in individual concealment. He complained of the necessity of combating the herd instinct: "Not only man and beast fall victim to it, tents and vehicles do so also." He complained at considerable length about both the bunching and symmetrical dispersal of tents and motor transport, sins to which the Germans were addicted. He also gave careful instructions on the construction of narrow, deep trenches, which must have no parapet and must be covered over, citing British positions as examples to be imitated. All armies were guilty of this need for orderliness and uniform alignment, a hopelessly entrenched peacetime ailment.

A heavily garnished US M4 Sherman tank barrels through a French village; an AFV camouflaged in this way would be difficult to detect from the air when it pulled over to a roadside against hedges or overhanging trees. The bracken and twigs are held on by wire or cord, but could easily get torn off when moving through dense brush. (Tom Laemlein/ Armor Plate Press)

46

British Churchill tanks of an infantry-support army tank brigade in Tunisia provide an almost textbook example of good siting and camouflage to avoid aerial observation. Lined up along the edge of a field of tall vegetation, they have been camouflaged with greenery cut from it, including upright branches. The turrets are partially covered with "shrimp net," but not the hulls, so that it does not snag in the tracks. (IWM NA17041)

## Reducing vehicle signature

However well sited a vehicle was, the tracks it left across the terrain could betray its position. Tracks were particularly telling in wet or muddy areas, deserts, and snow (and brushing out tracks with leafy limbs left the ground looking as if tracks had been brushed out with leafy limbs...).

Vehicle tracks were a major aid to aerial photo analysts in locating assembly areas, artillery positions, bivouacs, supply dumps, truck parks, and headquarters. The site or facility might be well camouflaged and vehicles parked beneath trees and drape-netted, but the tracks pointed a finger, and if there were multiple entrances and exits it was not difficult to identify the occupied area. Tracks were reduced by using existing roads and paths, avoiding cutting across open areas, and following natural terrain lines; paralleling existing tree lines, hedges, walls and fences; creating new roads into the area that were of the same pattern and style as local roads; avoiding cutting corners and shortcuts at road junctions, and using one-way traffic circulation. A track branching off a road to a wooded area could be made to continue past its actual end and on to join another road, with the turnoff into the woods concealed. Control measures were essential to ensure that drivers followed camouflage rules and traffic plan.

Reflection or shine was eliminated to the extent possible by covering windshields, windows, side mirrors, and headlights in daylight. Naturally, windshields could not be covered when driving, but they could be partly covered with mud, and overhanging foliage protruding beyond the cab roof shielded them from reflection. Jeeps and other vehicles had folding windshields, which were either removed, or folded down with canvas covers slipped on.

Distorting shadows and shapes was critical. The shadow cast by a vehicle's silhouette was just as valuable to photo analysts as being able to see the vehicle, betraying its presence and sometimes even its type. A vehicle's shape – whether a tank, assault gun, halftrack, scout car, or truck – was readily identifiable by anyone familiar with military vehicles, so distorting and breaking up its form to hamper ground and aerial observation was important. Disruptive pattern painting helped, as did nets, but for greater effect local vegetation had to be used. Shadows created on the vehicle itself were revealing; this was countered by parking vehicles beneath trees, among dense vegetation, against the shaded side of buildings or along some manmade or natural linear feature. A draped net or tarp was attached to the shaded side of the vehicle and sloped to the ground, and tree limbs and brush stacked on that side disrupted the shadow. Parking a vehicle where its shadow would fall among irregular vegetation or rubble also helped.

Distinctive shadows were cast by wheel wells, tires, track suspension systems, and bogie wheels. It was common practice when vehicles were halted or in position to drape tarps over wheel wells or lay boards or leafy limbs against them. Foliage could be propped against corners and fenders to break up straight lines; it was recommended that such low areas were painted a light color for counter-shading, but adhering mud and dirt countered this. Open crew compartments or cargo beds – especially with sidewalls or sideboards on trucks and halftracks, or any open-topped vehicle – cast deep shadows, and the same applied to trailers. Canvas tarps or camouflage nets could be draped over open compartments or cargo beds to eliminate such shadows. Canvas covers with supporting bows on cargo trucks provided more than weather protection; they eliminated shadows, and prevented the enemy from seeing what (if anything) was being carried. To further eliminate shadows the rear openings of covered cargo compartments were provided with back curtains. The US Army provided bows and canvas covers for fuel and water trucks, wreckers, bridge transport trucks, and water trailers – all valuable targets – to make them look more like normal cargo vehicles, but these seem to have been little used.

## Vehicle painting

US Army FM 5-20B, *Camouflage of Vehicles*, describes the main principles of vehicle painting:

> The enemy will usually see vehicles at an angle. At least two adjoining surfaces will be visible to him at once. For example, from close-range ground observation he might see a side and the front; from the air, or on an aerial photograph, he might see the top, a side, and the front. For this reason, vehicle patterns are designed to disrupt the cube shape of vehicles from all angles, to disrupt shadows cast by tarpaulin bows, to tie in with the shadow at the rear of a vehicle when it is faced into the sun, to tie in with the large dark shadow areas of windows, mudguards, wheels, and undercarriage, and to be bold enough to be effective at a distance.
>
> Patterns are composed of a light color and a dark color. Black or olive drab have proved satisfactory dark colors in several theaters of operations. The light color is selected to match a light color typical of and predominant in the terrain in which the vehicle operates. White or light gray paint is applied to the undersurfaces of vehicles to cause them to reflect light, thus lightening the dark shadows of the undercarriage. This is called counter-shading.
>
> Camouflage painting is not a cure-all. Alone, it cannot be relied on to do more than render a vehicle obscure, making it hard for an enemy gunner to locate the vehicle and confusing him as to the location of vulnerable points. Nor can it conceal a moving vehicle,

as dust, reflections, and motion itself will betray its presence. However, camouflage painting is a valuable supplement to other camouflage measures. Camouflage painting, along with good siting, dispersion, camouflage discipline, and the use of nets and drapes, increases the benefits to be derived from these measures. Together, and intelligently used, they will provide a high degree of concealment for any vehicle.

Points in developing camouflage patterns included:

- Background determines the colors to use.
- Undersurfaces should be lighter than upper surfaces.
- Patterns should be large and bold, cutting across the main straight lines of the piece.
- Patterns should be continued across adjacent surfaces, for example from horizontal to vertical.
- Colors used should contrast strongly.
- Black should be used sparingly, except in terrain which contains many deep shadows.

Camouflaging vehicles, regardless of the means, had benefits other than simply "hiding" them. Even partial camouflage on a vehicle might delay its being detected as a target or threat for valuable moments; could prevent its positive identification ("Is that a Mk III or Mk IV?"); and could make it difficult to estimate its range and its angle of perspective, and thus to take aim at vulnerable points.

A sophisticated example of the British use of decoys, and altering a vehicle's "signature," in North Africa. A convincing dummy Crusader tank, built with plywood and painted canvas over a light truck, tows a weighted trolley fitted with lengths of track to create convincing signs of its passage. Before the second battle of El Alamein, the Camouflage Unit under Col Geoffrey Barkas made 600 tanks "disappear" under dummy trucks, and "reappear" elsewhere. This was achieved in just 25 days, between September 27 and October 23, 1942. (IWM MH20772)

Allied AFV crewmen would say that the camouflage was to protect them just as much from their own over-eager airmen as from the enemy. Regardless of color finishes and tactical markings, all sides experienced attacks by their own airmen, who had a propensity to dive on any moving vehicle. The Allies often used red, orange, or yellow marker panels, while the Germans and Italians frequently used large national flags. Marker panels and flags were laid over truck hoods, atop tank turrets or on engine decks. Ambulances bore large Geneva Convention red crosses, usually on a white square backing for the Western Allies and a white disc for the Germans, Russians and early-war British ambulances. None of these measures could ever be relied upon to deter trigger-happy pilots.

Most countries used some shade of dark green or olive drab as their vehicle base color; OD represented a compromise between earth colors and foliage colors in temperate climates. Sand and tan shades were used for the base color in desert regions. Canvas cargo truck and trailer covers were sometimes painted in disruptive patterns, but this was frowned upon, as it could cause deterioration of the fabric. Sometimes large-caliber gun barrels were counter-shaded along the bottom in white or other light colors to reduce the darkness of the underside shadow.

The US Army's Specification 3-1 was issued in 1920, with changes and additions made over the years. Different shades of paint were used, varying due to the same colors being issued in lusterless (matt), semi-gloss, glossy, aircraft dope, enamels, and lacquers. While OD was the vehicle base color, actual shades varied greatly over time. The Army Air Forces used a darker shade of OD than the Ground Forces. Departmental responsibility for paints changed during the war, from Quartermaster to Engineers to Ordnance, and this resulted in shade changes. Additionally, owing to pigment shortages, different mixing procedures, and shortages of official color cards, vehicle and equipment manufacturers finished their products using slightly different shades.

British vehicle camouflage underwent a number of changes in both base colors and disruptive pattern schemes. Specific color schemes were specified for the UK, NW Europe, North Africa, Sicily, Italy, the Middle East, and Far East. Commonwealth forces used colors similar to the British, but different shades were used in their homelands to match local coloration, and some of these may have been retained overseas. Units were usually issued standard British colors in the UK or in-theater. Shades and disruptive patterns varied. In 1942, for example, Australia used dark green, khaki green, and light earth; 1943 saw the use of a two-color scheme of khaki green and sandy yellow, the latter being more yellow than British sand. Also during 1943 colors termed vehicle (medium) green and vehicle light gray were adopted, but were soon replaced with dark gray, dark green, and medium green. Medium green was achieved by mixing 50-50 dark gray and dark green.

The Germans used gray (*grau*) for AFVs, but a greenish shade of field gray (*feldgrau*) for other vehicles. From early 1943 the standard factory base color was changed to dark yellow (*dunkelgelb*), over which to paint darker green and brown camouflage patterns. In North Africa the Germans also used Italian, Luftwaffe, and captured British paints. German colors were standardized by a state agency, *Reichsausschuß für Lieferbedingungen und Gütesicherung* (National Committee for Quality Assurance and Delivery), standard RAL 840 R.

The Italians used sand yellow (*sabbia*) as a base color in Africa, Sicily, and Italy. Vehicles might be solid color, or in Africa be overpainted with varied red-brown (*terracotta*) disruptive patterns. In Sicily and Italy gray-green (*grigio verde*) and red-brown were used for pattern-painting. In the Balkans and Russia the base color was gray-green, sometimes with red-brown and/or sand-yellow patterns. There were no standardized patterns. Whitewash (*calce*) was used in the Russian winter.

| US Army Specification 3-1, vehicle camouflage colors | |
| --- | --- |
| No. 1 light green | No. 8 earth red |
| No. 2 dark green | No. 9 olive drab |
| No. 3 sand | No. 10 black |
| No. 4 field drab | No. 11 white |
| No. 5 earth brown | No. 12 forest green |
| No. 6 earth yellow | No. 13 desert sand |
| No. 7 loam | |

| British Standard vehicle colors B.S. designation | | |
| --- | --- | --- |
| **B.S. designation** | **Shade number** | **Comments** |
| *NW Europe:* | | |
| dark earth | No. 1A B.S. 987C | |
| khaki brown | No. 2 B.S. 987C | |
| khaki green | No. 3 B.S. 381 | a.k.a. bronze green (base color) |
| dark green | No. 5 B.S. 381 | |
| light green | | |
| *North Africa:* | | |
| slate grey | No. 34 B.S. 381 | |
| terra cotta | No. 44 B.S. 381 | deep red earth |
| light stone | No. 61 B.S. 381 | a.k.a. desert yellow |
| middle stone | No. 62 B.S. 381 | a.k.a. light mud |

As already mentioned, light blue and desert pink were used in North Africa. In Sicily, middle stone and black were used, and in Italy, khaki green No. 7 B.S. 381. In Malta a light stone base coat was overpainted with narrow, irregular black lines in a web pattern. There were also alternative shades similar to the standard shades.

| German standard vehicle colors | | |
| --- | --- | --- |
| **Farbe/RAL nummer** | **English** | **Comments** |
| *beige RAL 1001* | beige | Interior color sometimes used on exterior. |
| *oxidrot RAL 3009* | primer red | a.k.a. brick or dark red |
| *laubgrün RAL 6002* | leaf green | a.k.a. dark green |
| *olivgrün RAL 6003* | olive green | |
| *dunkelbraun RAL 7017* | dark brown | a.k.a. dark earth |
| *dunkelgrau RAL 7021* | dark gray | a.k.a. Panzer gray (principal base color) |
| *sandgrau RAL 7027* | sand gray | |
| *dunklelgelb RAL 7028* | dark yellow | a.k.a. sand yellow |
| *grünbraun RAL 8000* | green brown | a.k.a. *gelbbraun* (yellow brown), see RAL 8020 |
| *rotbraun RAL 8017* | red brown | a.k.a. *schokladenbraun* (chocolate brown) |
| *gelbbraun RAL 8020* | yellow brown | a.k.a. dark sand or *sandgelb* (sand yellow) |
| *weiss RAL 9002* | white | |

## Snow camouflage

Just because it was winter in Europe did not mean that snow would fall. In western Germany and the Low Countries snow conditions are seldom constant. Northern Germany was often free of snow; the further south one moved to higher elevations, snow was more constant – the opposite of snow conditions in America. Most of Eastern Europe and Russian were snowbound all winter; Moscow was at the same latitude as Hudson's Bay in Canada.

The terrain was seldom entirely white; much of NW Europe was heavily populated, and the landscape was full of trees, brush, hedges, roads, fences, cultivated fields, outcroppings, streams, ditches, walls, rubble, and thawed areas. Vehicles and equipment could be sited next to or among the dark areas.

Vehicle and foot tracks in snow or frost obviously pointed to concealed positions. Tracks created shadow lines detectable at long ranges, and sharp turns were even more obvious. To make tracks less conspicuous they should follow shadow-casting terrain and manmade features, with all vehicles following the same track. As in non-snow conditions, efforts had to be made to distort or obscure shadows cast on the snow by static vehicles.

Frost and snow would freeze to vehicles and large equipment, aiding in camouflage. Bed linen and white tarps were used to cover them; while white, these usually contrasted with the snow, but might be effective from a distance. No matter how well a position might be camouflaged in the snow, the churned-up marks left by vehicles and troop activity attracted attention, and artillery muzzle blast blew away snow and left powder-burn marks.

Whitewash (German, *Sumpfkalk*; Russian, *pivestkovii rastvor*; British, a.k.a. limewash) was widely used for camouflaging vehicles, helmets, and equipment in snow conditions. Whitewash is made from slaked lime (calcium hydroxide) and water, and is cheap to use; a 25kg (55lb) bag of lime makes about twice that weight in whitewash. A substitute was chalk dissolved in water. When winter snows appeared, vehicles and other equipment were completely or partly overpainted. Whitewash provided a matt texture, but was not very durable. It required several days to harden effectively or it rubbed off when running through vegetation and when crewmen clambered about on it. Powdered paste or salt was added so it would adhere better. Whitewashed vehicles blended well into winter fog and mist, especially among trees and brush.

In areas with evergreen vegetation it was common to only partly whitewash vehicles, leaving 10–15 percent of the original paint exposed, or to splotch it with a small amount of dark green or black. Dappled whitewash might be applied in areas where snow fell lightly, thawed, and fell again. As winter wore on and spring emerged much of the whitewash had worn off, exposing more of the original paint, so the vehicle's appearance "adapted itself" to the greener vegetation as the snow disappeared. Eventually the remaining whitewash had to be laboriously scrubbed off, or the vehicle was repainted.

In January 1945, the Anglo-Canadian 21st Army Group issued a *Snow Camouflage Booklet*. This noted that "Rapid thaws may be expected and snow cover will not

This US M2A1 halftrack car has been whitewashed, with a few bands of disruptive black (or possibly dark green) paint applied. The track suspension was difficult to camouflage; worse, the black band painted across the wheel and tire here will create an eye-catching "pinwheel" effect when the vehicle is moving. (Tom Laemlein/Armor Plate Press)

necessarily be continuous over a wide area. Moreover, even in deep snow, buildings, woods and other features still provide dark backgrounds. White paint or other whitening agents should not, therefore, be used directly on vehicles and weapons, but only as a means of whitening materials to be put on them." It additionally directed that "White paint may be used, when practicable, on the underside of any tarpaulin [cargo truck cover] which can be reversed." White calico cloth was provided in 3ft-wide rolls to be cut into patches with strings attached, for use on artillery or other nets or for attachment to tank turrets, guns, other vehicles, and for general improvisation.

## Camouflage-painting mistakes

There was more to camouflage-painting than merely slapping on paints in the colors of earth and vegetation; mistakes were frequent, and the following are some of the most common:

- Painting vertical or diagonal bands at the same angle, and all of an equal or near-equal width, especially of consistently alternating colors; these drew attention by their uniformity and unnatural regularity.
- A uniform pattern over the whole of the vehicle created too regular an appearance, such as painting the front and rear corners of the vehicle in the same color. Opposing corners should be different colors, and the splotches/bands differently shaped.
- Painted splotches, spots, bands, squiggles, etc, whether large or small, needed to be of differing sizes and irregular in distribution and form. Patterns should be bold and simple.
- Painting a straight or wavy band around the edge of, for example, a gun shield or vehicle fender, whether directly on the edge or closely paralleling it, served only to advertise its regular shape. Painted bands and patches should "bleed" off vehicle edges.
- Painting a band of contrasting color across wheels, or painting them in two different colors, attracted further attention to moving vehicles by creating a pinwheel or "flickering" effect. It was better to paint wheels solid colors. Alternating the colors of bogie wheels also created too regular an appearance.
- Too high a ratio of light colors (unless matching the terrain) drew attention to a vehicle, and at night could reflect ambient light. When traveling down a road against a dark background or passing trees between the observer and the vehicle, a light finish attracted attention. A selection of excessively dark colors could have a similar effect.
- The use of glossy or even semi-gloss paint rather than a flat (matt) finish. Even matt paint can reflect light from certain angles, especially when wet.

While it cannot really be categorized as a mistake, it was very common for AFVs to be committed to combat in new areas while still wearing the patterns and colors chosen for the region from which they had deployed. Examples include British tanks arriving in Tunisia with UK colors, and tanks arriving in Sicily with desert camouflage. This was due to lack of time or the correct paints, or to an unwillingness to paint them before embarkation for security reasons, so as not to signal their next deployment.

Crewman of a US M36 tank destroyer applying white paint to the suspension with a spray gun after the first winter snows have fallen. It was more common to simply throw buckets of whitewash over the running gear, but it was hardly worth the effort anyway, since in wintertime the wheels and bogies were perpetually coated with mud. (Tom Laemlein/Armor Plate Press)

**ABOVE RIGHT**
This US M4 Sherman has been partly whitewashed using paint rollers, providing a reasonably effective pattern against the light snow coverage and mud. (Tom Laemlein/Armor Plate Press)

# CAMOUFLAGING GUN POSITIONS

Positions for artillery and other crew-served weapons (AT and AA guns, mortars, machine guns, etc) were difficult to conceal. They had to be sited where they had adequate fields of fire, and were accessible by prime movers and ammunition vehicles, and they generated flash, smoke, dust, and noise. Nearby vehicle parks, stockpiled ammunition, command posts, fire-direction centers, and crew activity all attracted attention. Field artillery, AA guns, and larger AT guns were difficult to conceal and required large camouflage nets; the larger the nets, the easier they were to detect, appearing as more unnatural patches among natural vegetation.

Siting or positioning of artillery was a major factor in its concealment or detection. In forested areas clearings from which to fire field artillery were often scarce. Imagination was necessary to pick alternative firing positions: guns lined up on the long axis of a road oriented in the necessary direction, or placed along river or lake shores, or in small clearings hidden by camouflage nets. Emplacements on open ground or on the forward edge of wood lines were obvious to forward observers directing counterbattery fire.

There was also a tendency to emplace artillery batteries in geometric formations, which attracted the eye. Most light and medium batteries had four guns – certain types had six, very heavy batteries might have two, and Commonwealth armies used eight-gun batteries (with two four-gun troops). Photo analysts were familiar with the number of pieces comprising their opponent's batteries; if they spotted one, they would search nearby for the rest, and a predictable layout aided their task. Batteries might be emplaced in squares, diamonds, straight or staggered lines, and concave or convex arcs. It was better to use an irregular layout tied into the terrain pattern. For example, in a relatively open, cultivated area a battery's four guns might be positioned with one at a fence corner, another at a "T" junction of two walls, a third beside a clump of brush and saplings, and the fourth between two haystacks. However, the battery's guns could not be too widely dispersed, because they had to be close enough together to provide an overlapping concentration of fire – 20–40yds apart at the most.

Antiaircraft batteries were particularly conspicuous, as geometrically laid out positions improved fire concentrations. They had to be in broad, open areas for adequate fields of fire (they needed a lot of sky to track an aircraft across), and the guns were accompanied by a considerable amount of associated equipment – command post, fire control center, fire control predictor/director, sound detectors, searchlights, power generator, and perhaps radar. Light AA guns and machine-gun positions protecting against low-level attacks were often present, along with the usual crew quarters and ammunition dumps. In searching for AA positions, photo analysts knew to search outward from prospective bomber targets.

Artillery, AA and AT guns were easily recognizable from the air owing to their barrels, shields, and long trails or "spider mounts" (AA guns); these barrels and shields cast distinctive shadows. Their wheels were also noticeable from oblique angles, though this might be countered by draping tarps over the wheels and laying brush or boards against them. Dug-in gun positions were also large, usually of uniform shape, and with fairly high, thick parapets. Tracks left by the prime-movers positioning the weapons and the ammunition delivery vehicles also called attention to the position.

For relatively small artillery pieces a gun position could be cleared within a stand of small trees and large saplings; with the weapon emplaced, thin trees and saplings could be bent over the position and their tops wired together to create a camouflaging screen (this usually required a ladder, however). Nets had to cover not only the gun, but its parapet, the trenches and foxholes sheltering crew and gun equipment, the stacked ready-ammunition, expended shell cases, and packing materials. Typically the net extended further to the gun's rear than the front in order to cover all these. Prime-movers, support vehicles, and additional ammunition should have been parked well to the rear – ideally 300–500 yards, but, realistically, more often within 100 yards.

Besides muzzle-flash and smoke, firing also disturbed the ground in front of the muzzle. The result was burn marks, blasted-away vegetation, churned-up ground, and drifting dust. Even damp ground was dried out by frequent muzzle blasts, whether artillery or machine-gun; the soil would become crumbly,

A whitewashed US Sherman is ground-guided through a German village; the uncamouflaged tarps, crates and other stowage help break up its all-white silhouette in this urban setting. Note the simple and unobtrusive identification on the rear hull – a black hand-painted "4," visible from behind only. Possibly this company's 18 tanks were simply numbered in sequence. (Tom Laemlein/Armor Plate Press)

The African-American crew of a 155mm M1A1 howitzer of a field artillery battalion in a gun-pit in Normandy, August 1944. The flat-top net is heavily garnished, apparently with "bow-tie" strips leaving hanging ends; the side drape net has a sparser garnish in "U" shapes or "Greek key" pattern. (US Army)

moisture vapor rose if conditions were damp enough, and eventually dust was raised. For small weapons the ground could be kept wet (including by urination), and for larger ones it could be covered with planks, pegged-down tarps, split-open cardboard boxes, a layer of sandbags, or anchored sheet metal roofing. For artillery, stakes were driven into the ground around an area slightly larger than the blast-marked area; chicken wire was stretched between the stakes about a foot above the ground, and brush and weeds were spread over the wire (this needed to be replaced after each fire mission). Of course, any of these efforts might, in their turn, make the position more conspicuous.

Antitank gun positions presented particular problems. Larger AT guns were difficult to hide, especially their long barrels and distinctive squared shields. As tank armor improved, AT guns had to get larger, making it more difficult and time-consuming to dig them in and camouflage them. To survive the enemy's usually fast reaction, they had to be able to be moved rapidly to alternate or supplementary positions. (The distinction is that alternate positions cover the same field of fire or target area as the primary position, while supplementary positions cover another or secondary sector.) Natural cover and

**G** **TYPICAL CAMOUFLAGE-PAINTING MISTAKES**

**(1)** This Australian AEC Matador artillery tractor bears Middle East theater camouflage in slate gray and sand yellow. The diagonal bands, of uniform width and angle and repeated in a rigidly alternating pattern, are far too conspicuous. (Similar uniformly-wide vertical bands were even worse.) The windshield, side windows, headlights, reflectors and side mirrors all reflect sunlight.

**(2)** This *Typ 82 Kübelwagen* field car is painted with a pattern of uniformly small dark green spots on a sand-color base. These are neither large enough, nor irregular enough, to be effective at any range; from even a short distance the finish will appear as a solid color – against which the black-and-white *Balkenkreuz* stands out.

**(3)** The dark yellow shield of this German 8.8cm PaK 43/41 *"Scheunetor"* ("barn door") antitank gun has been overpainted with a red-brown pattern that parallels the edges, and thus highlights the regular shape of the shield. The pattern should run off the edges at random angles and intervals.

**(4)** A rare example of Red Army vehicle camouflage-painting, and an incompetent one. The rear wheel of this BA-64B *Bobik* armored car is painted halved in two contrasting colors, while the front wheel is divided by a narrow bar. Either one of these will create a flickering "pinwheel" effect when the car is moving – which will negate the care taken to paint the red star inconspicuously small.

**(5)** This Nissen hut on an RAF airfield in the UK is a prime example of the unthinking application of centrally prescribed patterns. The large, baldly-contrasting pattern might make it more difficult for an attacking pilot to identify the structure and estimate his range when closing at speed, but it hardly "hides" the building. The windows have black-out curtains inside, but the glass outside would reflect the sun brightly. Finally, the alignment of the building has been carefully signaled by whichever military genius ordered the whitewashed rocks arranged as kerbstones along the tracks.

This 105mm M7B1 self-propelled howitzer of US 7th Armd Div is positioned on an earth ramp to increase its elevation for long-range fire; the SP howitzer mount only allowed half the elevation of the towed weapon. An ungarnished "shrimp net" is draped over and around the position, but the careless scatter of black shell packing tubes and pale natural wood boxes would still draw attention to it. (Tom Laemlein/Armor Plate Press)

concealment was used as much as possible, as well as manmade features such as walls, rubble, the interior of buildings, haystacks, and log piles. It was common to hide guns in such concealment and then place brush, rocks, or boards to disguise the shield and tires. A few weapons were manufactured with "misshapen" or wavy-edged shields, namely the German 3.7cm PaK 35/36 AT gun and 7.5cm leIG 18 infantry gun. Some US units fastened sheet metal strips cut to a wavy edge across the top of the shield of 37mm M3A1 AT guns.

Digging-in mortars was easier, since they were relatively small and man-portable. Being indirect-fire weapons, they were often positioned out of the enemy's line-of-sight, and their angle of fire made them easier to conceal from ground-level observation. In more mobile situations or for short-term defense, rather than digging-in mortars they were often simply set up behind walls or buildings, in ditches or gullies, or behind anything else that would offer cover.

Machine guns naturally had to be set up where they had an effective field of fire, and so were vulnerable to all forms of direct fire. In the defense they were extremely valuable, and the protection they were given in the form of bunkers and pillboxes was often out of proportion to their size. Efforts were made to reduce muzzle flash and dust to further conceal their location. It was emphasized that, whether in defense or attack, machine gun crews should avoid setting up near easily-described points of reference in the landscape, to make it harder for enemy observers to direct fire at the position.

The Russians often issued ungarnished nets, including actual commandeered fishing nets, on which clumps of grass, weeds, or small branches were laid. Here one has been erected over an obsolete 76.2mm M1902/30 field gun. (Nik Cornish at www.Stavka.org.uk)

# MISCELLANEA

## Observation posts

Artillery observation posts needed to be positioned so as to bring large areas under surveillance, and needed to have multiple avenues of approach. By definition, OPs needed to be on higher ground, but obvious positions were avoided: hilltops, ridge crests, church steeples, the tallest buildings, lone farmhouses on a hillside, etc. The enemy might take such possible OP sites under speculative fire, so less obvious sites were selected: the upper floors of two-story and higher buildings, but not necessarily the highest floor; in attics with observation holes knocked through the roof; inside an already-destroyed farmhouse, and so on. Sometimes actual OPs were established near obvious OP sites to distract the enemy. OPs exhibited many identifying signs that had to be hidden: radio antennas, telephone lines, map boards, binoculars and telescopes (which could reflect sunlight), and personnel activity. Even if the enemy did not identify OPs exactly enough to fire on them their general location might be fairly obvious, and smoke rounds might be fired into that area to blind them.

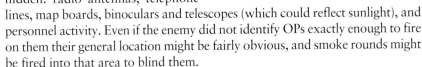

## Obstacles

It is virtually impossible to camouflage obstacles, but some measures were available to delay their detection, if the terrain and tactical situation permitted. While obstacles were critical to the defense, their presence alerted analysts to the fact that defensive positions were nearby and within range to cover the obstacles. A study of the terrain on the enemy side, even if his positions were ideally camouflaged, could identify likely positions.

Barbed wire obstacles and tripwires could be emplaced among brush and high grass, as well as on low ground or behind reverse slopes, and gaps for friendly patrols had to be concealed. Roadblocks and tank obstacles could be positioned around bends and curves to surprise advancing tankers. Antitank and antipersonnel minefields were buried, but experienced troops often detected them owing to mounded or disturbed earth, improper replacement of ground cover, soil discoloration, shallow depressions after rain, tripwires, and discarded mine packing materials and arming pins. In the desert the wind could blow the sand off and expose mines. Mine warning signs and strung wire were placed on the rear edge of minefields to warn their own troops. It should be noted that often mines were simply laid on the ground fully exposed with no concern for camouflage, their mere presence being expected to deter the enemy. This method was only effective if covered by fire.

**TOP**
British 2-pdr antitank gun during coastal exercises in England, 1940–41. Its low profile makes it easy to camouflage effectively with natural materials – here, thick gorse bushes; but since the wheels have been removed from the carriage for firing, it will be more difficult to move quickly to an alternate position – a necessity of survival for AT-gun crews.

**ABOVE**
Soviet 45mm M1930 AT gun emplaced in a snow-covered ravine, effectively camouflaged with a sheet and piled snow. (Nik Cornish at www.Stavka.org.uk)

## Decoys

The "reverse" of camouflage was decoys or dummies. These could be effective in distracting and misleading the enemy as to a force's actual strength, limitations, and dispositions, and might also attract fire away from actual positions and facilities. Decoys could not be too obvious, and had to at least appear to be plausibly sited and camouflaged. Elaborate, large-scale deceptions required such specialty equipment as canvas-and-plywood fake truck bodies mounted over tanks ("wolves in sheeps' clothing"), or fake tanks mounted over trucks, and rubber inflatable tanks ("sheep in wolves' clothing"). The British made widespread use of both types of decoy in North Africa, where the open terrain made enemy aerial reconnaissance a real danger, and the deployment of armor on the coastal or desert flanks was a critical calculation. Large numbers of rubber Shermans also played their part in the successful Allied deception plan before D-Day.

This battery of four Soviet 152mm M1938 howitzers have been whitewashed and dug into packed-snow emplacements. The shadows cast within the gun pits and the extensively churned-up snow around the positions attract attention, especially at early morning and nightfall when the sunlight is flat. (Nik Cornish at www.Stavka.org.uk)

Less well known are the decoy Matilda tanks used by the British in France in 1939–40, and the fake Panthers used by the Germans in Normandy in 1944. These "tactical-level" dummies were mostly made from local materials and were quick and easy to erect. Unless a unit occupied an area for a significant period there was little time available for erecting decoys, which required a good deal of manpower and materials, often for little return. However, the US Army's FM 5-20D, *Camouflage of Field Artillery*, provided general guidance that applied equally to other decoy efforts:

> Except when we are trying to mislead the enemy as to our strength and intentions, true positions must be concealed before decoys are set in place, because a decoy is effective only when there is no evidence of the object to which it is related.
>
> The decoy position should be located to one flank of the firing battery to avoid possible hits on the latter during enemy adjustment

---

**H**  **ARTILLERY BATTERY POSITION**

This reconstructs the layout of a German battery of horse-drawn 10.5cm leFH 18 light howitzers during mobile operations in France, 1940. Rather than emplace the battery's four howitzers **(1, 2, 3 & 4)** in a geometric pattern, as used in peacetime training exercises, it was safer to disperse them irregularly, positioned beside natural or manmade features so that they did not stand out starkly against the background or the terrain patterns. Long-range observers and photo interpreters might miss them in a quick search, and even if they detected one or more of the guns or pieces of associated equipment an irregular pattern of dispersal might hamper them in trying to locate the rest. The guns were roughly camouflaged by having shelter-quarters draped over the wheels and branches laid against the shields **(inset)**, which at least broke up distinctive shapes; however, guns, vehicles and horse teams all left distinctive tracks across the ground. One deception technique was for one of the howitzers

to be employed as a roving gun (*Arbeitsgeschütz*), firing from alternate positions 250–300 yards from the battery. In this way it could conduct harassing fires, and any return fire would not affect the main battery. Here the No.4 gun is returning to its position.

Besides the guns the 120-man battery had 4 caissons, 8 limbers, 15 wagons, and more than 100 horses, all of which had to be kept well clear of the guns to avoid counterbattery fire – the horses furthest away, since they were the most vulnerable. The caissons are with the guns, but the limbers and wagons are lined up in the shelter of tree and hedge lines (upper left). The damaged farm buildings house the battery HQ, troop quarters, equipment and stores. The forward observation post would be a considerable distance away, and connected by field-telephone wire. When there was an enemy armor threat, AT mines were laid on the roads and intersections approaching the position from the front and flanks.

on the decoy. The exact distance between the two positions depends upon the local situation. The maximum distance should be small enough to confuse the enemy in his attempts to correlate sound- and flash-ranging data with results of his visual observation.

The principal intentional 'mistakes' to make in preparing a decoy position are those which would be typical at an actual position improperly concealed – evidence of blast marks, foot and vehicle tracks, regular spacing of pieces, debris, foxholes and special trenches, spoil, communication wire dug in across roads, and shell cases.

However, *the simulation must not be overdone.* The decoy position must be discovered through relatively slight clues. A decoy position is convincing if a few tracks are allowed to show just outside the position, if light paths appear to lead to aiming posts, if a few cans are tossed into the open near a woods where a kitchen might logically operate. Another effective ruse is to arrange piles of brush in a regular pattern to simulate piles of ammunition…

An evacuated position can become an effective decoy position, particularly if some old flat-tops remain on the site. For the decoy to be completely effective, some signs of activity must be maintained. New tracks and paths should be made from time to time. Blast marks should be emphasized and new ones added. The decoy's effectiveness should be verified by aerial observation and photography."

Logs, lumber, scrap metal, canvas, destroyed vehicles and equipment, and anything else found locally could be used as decoy materials. Foot-deep foxholes and trenches could be dug, the low parapets partly camouflaged with leaves and ground-cover materials; the appearance of depth was enhanced by placing brush, limbs, and leaves, especially dark-colored, in the holes/trenches and crushing them down. There were instances when scarecrow-like dummy troops were emplaced. In an Italian sector a post was found manned with straw-filled dummies in German uniforms stripped from corpses.

# CONCLUSIONS

There is little doubt that the many tactical camouflage disciplines and techniques were important to combat units in World War II. Their effectiveness is difficult to assess, as so many techniques were applied by units with widely varying degrees of proficiency. Success depended greatly on the emphasis placed on such efforts by commanders and on the discipline and initiative of the troops. Unit training did not always emphasize camouflage; it was when units met the enemy that its importance became obvious and efforts increased, especially when the enemy possessed aerial reconnaissance.

Today, in parallel with new light-amplification vision and thermal imaging devices, there have been improvements in camouflage fabrics to reduce the effectiveness of such technologies. Camouflage paints have also been improved in durability, resistance to fading, and infrared absorption to reduce the detection of vehicles at night. Camouflage nets are still effective, but have been much improved by the use of plastics, which make them lighter, easier to erect, infrared-absorbing, non-water-absorbing, and longer lasting. Even so, many materials and most basic techniques used in World War II are still in use, and the study of World War II camouflage practices is still worthwhile for modern armies.

# FURTHER READING

It must be noted that some of the commercial books here address pre-Normandy strategic deception operations, and provide little on tactical camouflage at division level and below.

Bertin, François, *D-Day Normandy: Weapons – Uniforms – Military Equipment* (Drexel Hill, PA; Casemate, 2007)

Culver, Bruce, *Panzer Colors, Vol. 1, 2, and 3: Camouflage of the German Panzer Forces, 1939–1945* (Carrolton, TX; Squadron/Signal Publications, 1976, 1978, & 1984)

Gawne, Jonathan, *Ghosts of the ETO: American Tactical Deception Units in the European Theatre, 1944–1945* (Drexel Hill, PA; Casemate, 2002)

Hartcup, Guy, *Camouflage: The History of Concealment and Deception in War* (Barnsley, UK; Pen & Sword, 2008)

Reit, Seymour, *Masquerade: The Amazing Camouflage Deceptions of World War II* (Portland, OR; Hawthorn Books, 1978)

Stanton, Shelby, *US Army Uniforms of World War II* (Harrisburg, PA; Stackpole, 1991)

Zaloga, Steven J., *Blitzkrieg: Armor Camouflage & Markings, 1939–1940 (Belgium, France, Germany, Italy, Netherlands, Poland, Soviet Union)* (Carrolton, TX; Squadron/Signal Publications, 1984)

Military Training Pamphlet No.46, *Camouflage Part 1: General Principles: Equipment and Materials (all Arms)* (British & Commonwealth)

The US Army issued a comprehensive series of field manuals on camouflage; copies of these may be purchased from Military/Info Publishing, http://www.military-info.com/Index.htm:

FM 5-15 *Field Fortifications* (also addresses camouflage)

FM 5-20 *Camouflage, Basic Principles*

FM 5-20A *Camouflage of Individuals and Infantry Weapons*

FM 5-20B *Camouflage of Vehicles*

FM 5-20C *Camouflage of Bivouacs, Command Posts, Supply Points, and Medical Installations*

FM 5-20D *Camouflage of Field Artillery*

FM 5-20E *Camouflage of Aircraft on the Ground and Airdromes*

FM 5-20F *Camouflage of Antiaircraft Artillery*

FM 5-20G *Camouflage of Rear Areas and Fixed Fortifications*

FM 5-20H *Camouflage Materials and Manufacturing Techniques*

TM 5-269 *Materials for Protective Concealment*

A British 25-pdr gun-howitzer and ammunition limber towed by a Morris Quad, composed entirely of dummies. They would appear authentic in aerial photos, and in suitable lighting conditions could deceive ground observers down to between 500 and 1,000 yards. (IWM H42529)

# INDEX